PHILIPPIANS
A Remedy for the Spiritual "Blahs"!

Dr. Ian A. Fair

HCU Media LLC
Accra, Ghana ◊ Frisco, TX

PHILIPPIANS
A COMMENTARY AND STUDY GUIDE ON PAUL'S ESPISTLE TO THE PHILIPPIANS

HCU Media LLC

Published and Copyright © 2019
By Dr. Ian A. Fair & HCU Media LLC

ISBN-13: 978-1-939468-11-6 (Paperback Edition)

Also available in Kindle form

Printed in the USA

ALL RIGHTS RESERVED
No part of this publication may be reproduced, stored in a retrieval system, or transmitted in any form by any means – electronic, mechanical, photocopying, recording or otherwise – without prior written consent.

Scripture quotations, unless otherwise noted, are from The Holy Bible, Revised Standard Version, copyright 1971, Zondervan Bible Publishers.

Cover Design by Dale Henry – www.dalehenrydesign.com

First Edition September 2019
10 9 8 7 6 5 4 3 2 1

TABLE OF CONTENTS

Philippians:
A Remedy for the Spiritual "Blahs"!

TABLE OF CONTENTS 0

Preface 1

Bibliography 3

Chapter 1: The Four Pauline Prison Epistles 5

Chapter 2: Paul's Epistolary Style 19

Chapter 3: Salutation and Laudatio Prayer 27

Chapter 4: Paul's Present Circumstances and a Suitable Philippian Response 39

Chapter 5: Jesus Christ Our Model for Christian Service 51

Chapter 6: Paul's Encouragement to the Philippians to Mature in their Christian Witness 73

Chapter 7: Paul's Exhortations for the Philippians 83

Chapter 8: Paul's Theology in a Nutshell! 93

Chapter 9: Paul's Final Exhortations to the Philippians. 115

AUTHOR 145

WHO WE ARE 147

Preface

This study is not intended to be an extensive scholarly exegetical commentary on Paul's Epistle to the Philippians. Primarily it was written to provide resources for the serious Bible student or leader of a Bible study group in the Epistle of Philippians. However, it is also intended to go beyond the normal level of Bible study guide in that it will include references to the original language of the Epistle, Greek, with both the Greek alphabet and an English transliteration provided for those not familiar with the Greek.

Where necessary, or where I have felt the need for some scholarly comment, I have provided quotes from some of the leading scholars in the Epistle to the Philippians, or on Paul's theology. Some of the quotes are fairly long and I beg the indulgence of the reader with the request that the reader work through these quotes as I believe the time spent will in the long run prove helpful. Another reason for my including extensive quotes is that the primary readership I have in mind are ministers and church leaders in Africa who do not have many of the scholarly resources readily at hand. If further reading is necessary they can with some effort obtain the original source.

I have resisted the temptation to reference too many Greek-English Lexicons and have limited my references mostly to Spiros Zodhiates' excellent *Complete Word Study Dictionary: New Testament*. On occasion I have referenced Gerhard Kittel's *Theological Dictionary of the New Testament*.

It will not take the reader long to discover that I appreciate the balanced and scholarly research and writing of Dr. Peter T. O'Brien of Australia; of Dr. Gordon D. Fee; Drs. Gerald Hawthorne and Ralph P. Martin; Dr. Moisés Silva; and Dr. Norman Tom Wright.

I have occasionally included extended excerpts from some select scholars such as Peter O'Brien, Gordon Fee, Gerald Hawthorne and others as convenient resources to the study. This does not say that there are not useful comments from other fine scholars, but then, I have already explained that this study is not intended to be an exhaustive scholarly commentary. Nor do these references say that I agree with all that these scholars might say regarding Pauline theology. However, I do recommend the works listed in the bibliography as a good foundation to the study of the Epistle to the Philippians.

Bibliography

Greek-English Lexicons (Dictionaries)

Friberg, Timothy, Barbara Friberg, Neva F. Miller, *Analytical Lexicon of The Greek New Testament,* Grand Rapids: Baker Books, 2000.
Kittel, Gerhard, Gerhard Friedrich, *Theological Dictionary of the New Testament*, Grand Rapids: Wm B. Eerdmans, 1964.
Zodhiates, Spiros, *The Complete Word Study Dictionary: New Testament*, Chattanooga: AMG International, 1993.

Dictionaries

The Anchor Bible Dictionary, Ed. David Noel Freedman, New York: Doubleday, 1992.
The International Standard Bible Encyclopedia, Ed. James Orr, *et al*, Grand Rapids: Wm B, Eerdmans, 1939, 2003.
Harper's Bible Dictionary, Paul Achtemeier, *et al*. Society of Biblical Literature, 1985.
Tyndale Bible Dictionary, Ed. Walter A. Ewell, *et al*, Carol Stream, Ill., Tyndale House, 2008.
Baker Encyclopedia of the Bible, Ed. Walter A, Ewell, Grand Rapids: Baker, 1988.

Introductions to the New Testament

Fee, Gordon D. and Douglas Stuart, *How to Read the Bible Book by Book*, Zondervan, 2002.
Holladay, Carl R., *A Critical Introduction to the New Testament*, Abingdon, 2005.
Johnson, Luke Timothy, *The Writings of the New Testament*, Fortress, 1999.

Commentaries and Theological Studies

Ash, Tony, *Philippians, Colossians, & Philemon*, Joplin: College Press, 1994.

Bloesch, Donald G., *Essentials of Evangelical Theology*, Vol. 2, New York: Harper and Row, 1978.

Caird, G. B. *Paul's Letters from Prison*, Oxford: Oxford University Press, 1976.

Carson, D. A. *Basics for Believers: An Exposition of Philippians*, Grand Rapids: Baker Publishing, 1996.

Fee, Gordon D., *Paul's Letter to the Philippians*, Grand Rapids: Wm B. Eerdmans, 1995.

Guthrie, Donald, *New Testament Theology,* Downers Grove: Inter-Varsity Press, 1981.

Hawthorne, Gerald, and Ralph P. Martin, *Philippians*, Word Biblical Commentary, Nashville: Thomas Nelson Publishers, 2004.

Loh, I-Jin, and Eugene A. Nida, *A Translator's Handbook on Paul's Letter to the Philippians*, New York: United Bible Societies, 1977.

Melick, Richard R. Jr., *Philippians, Colossians, Philemon*, Nashville: Broadman and Holman, 1991.

O'Brian, Peter T., *The Epistle to the Philippians,* Grand Rapids: Eerdmans, 2010.

Richardson, Alan, *A Dictionary of Christian Theology*, London: SCM Press, 1969.

Silva, Moisés, *Philippians*, Grand Rapids: Baker Academic, 2005.

Thielman, Frank S. *Philippians*, The NIV Application Commentary, Grand Rapids: Zondervan, 2009.

Wright, Norman Tom, *Paul for Everyone, The Prison Letters*, Louisville: Westminster John Knox Press, 2004.

Illustrations

Permission to use the map of the Via Egnatia and photos of the Via Egnatia were requested from their source with no response as of publication date.

Chapter 1: The Four Pauline Prison Epistles

Traditionally the four prison epistles, Ephesians, Colossians, Philippians, and Philemon have been considered to have been written by Paul from prison in Rome, ca CE 60-62 or 61-63. There is some debate as to where Paul was imprisoned, with Ephesus, Caesarea Philippi, or most likely Rome being the proposed site of Paul's imprisonment. Most scholars however consider Rome to be the most likely location for Paul's imprisonment. N. T. Wright, an excellent Pauline scholar, prefers Ephesus as the location of Paul's writing. We will however, concede to the views of many other good scholars and prefer Rome as the place of Paul's imprisonment and writing.

The circumstances leading to Paul's imprisonment in Rome were as follows; at Miletus (Acts 20:17) Paul called the elders of the church in Ephesus to meet with him. The text indicates that he might not see the elders of Ephesus again. Paul then left the Ephesian elders at Miletus and travelled toward Caesarea and Jerusalem (Acts 21:1-15). While in Jerusalem to deliver a benevolent gift from the Gentile churches to the church in Jerusalem (cf. 1 Cor 16:1; 2 Cor 8, 9; Rom 15:30) Paul was arrested (Acts 21:27) and tried by the Sanhedrin (Acts 23:1). When the Jews made a plot to kill Paul, a Roman Centurion transferred him to Caesarea to be tried by Felix, the Roman Governor of the region. Exercising his rights as a Roman citizen, Paul appealed his case to Caesar and was then shipped off to Rome. Carefully read Acts 24:1-25:12.

After arriving in Rome, he was placed in prison, or under house arrest, until his accusers arrived from Jerusalem. He was released after two years (according to Roman law) when his accusers did not arrive to bring charges against him.

While in prison in Rome, Paul had plenty of time to contemplate his missionary experiences and his ministry. It is most likely that it was during this time that Paul wrote the four Prison Epistles. In due course Paul was released from the Roman prison which apparently included some time spent in house arrest. Apparently during his house imprisonment, he was able to receive visitors to his house and to conduct a limited ministry of outreach.

For some reason, possibly the receipt of news and a gift from the church in Philippi, Paul wrote the letter to the Philippian church. This was most likely toward the end of his two-year imprisonment, ca CE 60-62.

As mentioned in my commentary on Ephesians some scholars are not comfortable with the Pauline authorship of two of the Prison Epistles, namely Ephesians and Colossians, but most accept the Pauline authorship of Philippians.

Comment on the Authorship of the Prison Epistles

The traditional view of the authorship of the four prison epistles is that they were written by the Apostle Paul. However, there are some scholars who question the Pauline authorship of Ephesians and Colossians, but this is not a universal opinion. These scholars consider either one or both Ephesians and Colossians to have been written by someone close to Paul, possibly by a fellow missionary.

The epistle regarding which most questions are raised is Ephesians. Reasons for questioning Ephesians are as follows: the impersonal nature of the epistle – it contains no personal greetings; the discussion relating to the church seems to manifest a later ecclesiastical perspective and development of the church than present during Paul's Roman imprisonment; a greater emphasis is given to the universal church; some of the language and terminology seems different from the accepted Pauline Epistles like Romans, Corinthians, and Galatians.

However, the fact that Ephesians was possibly not written to only one congregation with specific problems, and is seemingly a general or universal letter, raises questions and proposes answers to most of these negative assumptions. Note the comment by Peter T. O'Brien:

> There are, however, considerable difficulties with the approach of Milton and Lincoln (who question the Pauline authorship, IAF) to the literary relationship of Ephesians and Colossians. In our judgment, their conclusions raise more problems than they solve … It is inappropriate, therefore, to conclude that Ephesians is non-Pauline because of the author's use of Colossians … The view that Paul wrote both letters, as we shall endeavor to show, does greater justice to the evidence.[1]

---

[1] Peter T. O'Brien, *The Letter to the Ephesians*, Grand Rapids: Wm. B. Eerdmans, 1999, pp. 12ff.

We will, however, work with the view that all four of these epistles are Pauline, written by the Apostle Paul while in a Roman prison ca 60-63 CE. Cf. Luke Timothy Johnson, *The Writing of the New Testament*, 1999; Gordon D. Fee & Douglas Stuart, *How to Read the Bible Book by Book*, 2002; Norman Tom Wright, *Paul or Everyone, The Prison Letters*, 2004, Peter T. O'Brien, *The Letter to the Ephesians*, Grand Rapids: Wm. B. Eerdmans, 1999, Peter T. O'Brien, *Colossians, Philemon*, Word Biblical Commentary, Dallas: Word Books, 1982, Douglas J. Moo, *The Letter to Colossians and Philemon*, Grand Rapids: Wm. B. Eerdmans, 2008, and Gordon D. Fee, *Paul's Letter to the Philippians*, Grand Rapids: Wm. B. Eerdmans, 1995.[2]

---

[2] Cf. also Ian A. Fair, *Ephesians*, HCU Media, 2014, pp. 4, 5.

The City of Philippi:

For the geographic location of Philippi in the Roman province of Macedonia note the map below. Philippi is at the top center of the map.

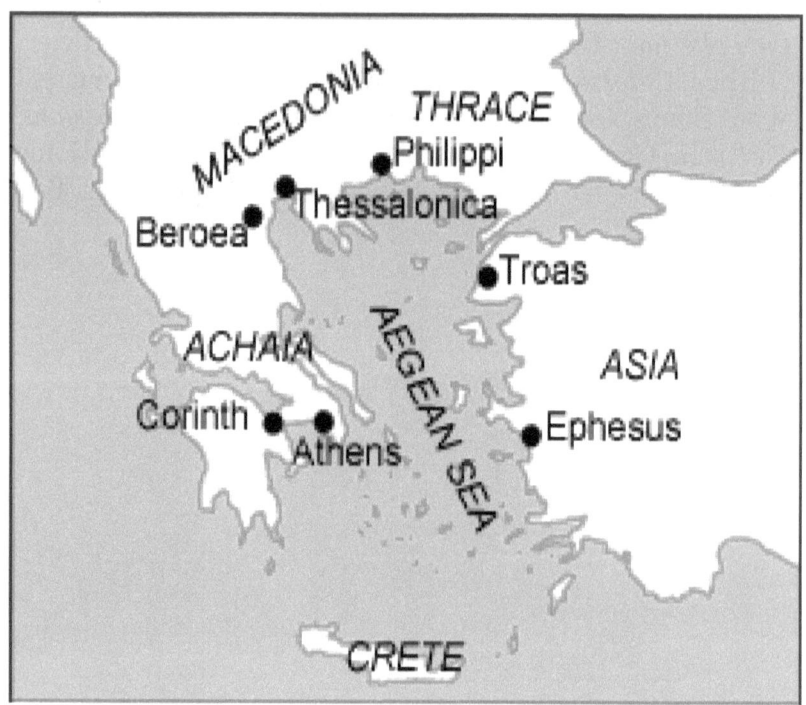

Permission to use map granted by Bible History Online

The City of Philippi had been established by Philip II, King of Macedon in 356 BCE. It eventually became a favored city of Caesar Augustus and was granted Roman colonial and monetary favors. It stood on the major thoroughfare and road, the *Via Egnatia* that ran from Rome in the west to Byzantium (Istanbul) in the east.

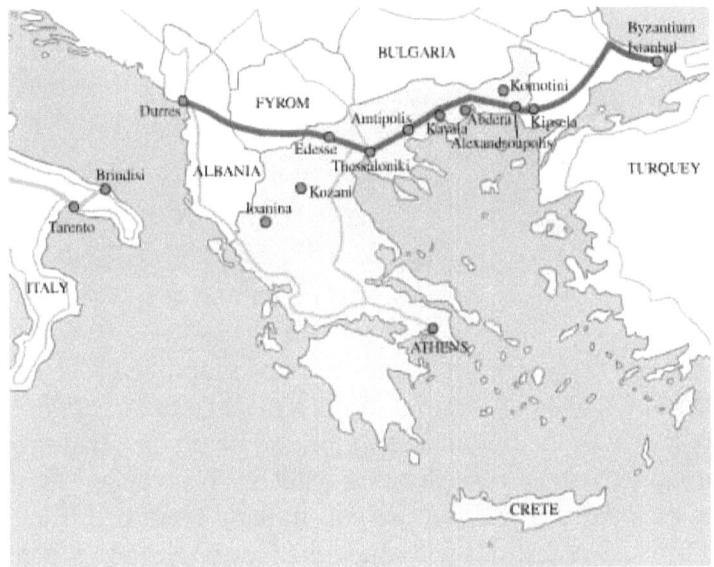

Map of Egnatian Way – *Via Egnatia*

Egnatian Way

Road Sign on Egnatian Way

Philippi lay 9 miles inland from the seaport of Neapolis. By the time Paul arrived in Philippi it was a major city of significant importance to the region and Rome and being on a major traffic thoroughfare East to West along what has been called the Egnatian Way or Via Egnatia. It was also a strategic crossroad from the Aegean Sea in the South to Macedonia in the North. Philippi was an important and strategic center, culturally, philosophically, commercially, and militarily.

The *Baker Encyclopedia of the Bible* has the following interesting article on Philippi:

> Philippi gained worldwide fame in 42 BC. when the imperial armies of Antony and Octavian defeated the Republican generals Brutus and Cassius (the assassins of Julius Caesar). The victory opened the way for the emergence of the Roman Empire under the rule of Octavian (Augustus).
>
> Veterans from the war of 42 BC. and other battles commonly settled in Philippi. When Paul came to the city it still reflected its Latin/military heritage. Situated on the Ignatian Way it was one stop on that great military highway connecting the Adriatic with the Aegean. It possessed a distinct civic pride inasmuch as it was a Roman colony (enjoying numerous privileges such as tax exemptions), promoted Latin as its official language, and hosted numerous Roman citizens. Its government was modeled on the municipal

constitution of Rome (its leader bearing Roman titles throughout) and the people lived as if they were indeed located in Italy. As Luke records in Acts 16:21, the citizens viewed themselves as "Romans."

Paul visited the city on his second missionary tour and years later wrote one letter to the church. The account of Acts gives detailed attention to Paul's visit. The narrative frequently refers to the city's Roman heritage: not only does Paul successfully employ his Roman citizenship in his defense (16:36), but the city magistrates bear the dignified Latin title *Praetor* ...

There appears to have been a small Jewish community here. The church began with believing Jewish women who met outside the city because there was no synagogue. Later they convened in the home of an important woman convert named Lydia (16:14, 15, 40).

Some have suggested that Luke may have had a special interest in Philippi. This is explained not only by his careful attention to the city, but by the "we" sections of Acts. The first "we" section (when Luke joins Paul) begins and ends at Philippi (16:10, 40). This suggests that Luke stayed behind in the city after Paul's departure. Then on the third tour Luke joins Paul again when the apostle passes through Philippi (20:6).

Archaeological evidence of Christianity has been found at the ruins of Philippi (modern Filibedjik).[3]

The Church at Philippi

Acts 16:6: Paul's Second Mission Journey (ca. CE 49-52):

On his second mission journey Paul and his companions travelled up the western region of the Roman province of Asia in the area of Mysia. Paul was "forbidden" to "speak the word in Asia" hoping eventually then to move over from Mysia into the region of Bithynia. We do not know how the message of the Holy Spirit forbidding him to speak in Asia (which included the regions of Mysia and Bithynia) was conveyed to Paul but Luke informs us that God through the Holy

---

[3] Elwell, W. A., & Beitzel, B. J. "Philippi," *Baker Encyclopedia of the Bible*, Grand Rapids: Baker Book House, 1988, vol. 2, pp. 1676f.

Spirit did not intend Paul to go in that direction, so they went to the coastal city of Troas in Mysia. While in Troas Paul had a remarkable vision from God.

Acts 16:9: The Vision of the Man from Macedonia:

In this vision a man from the Roman province of Macedonia appeared to Paul inviting him to travel to Macedonia and preach the gospel in Macedonia. Three interesting facts surface here! *One*, this would be Paul's first entrance into what we now call Europe. *Second*, Macedonia was the home of Alexander the Great (ca 356-323 BCE) who had conquered most of the region east of the Mediterranean Sea as far south as Egypt and East as India. Alexander had Hellenized that part of the world to where Greek had become the common language of the region, thus facilitating the spread of the Gospel in the 1st century CE. *Third*, this narrative of Acts 16 is important since it introduces Luke into the story of Acts in what has become known as the "we" passages in which Luke inserts himself into the narrative! Note Acts 16:11, *"Setting sail therefore from Troas, we made a direct voyage to Samothrace..."* The "we" passages engage Luke in the experience of Paul's group in Philippi. We assume from this that Philippi may have been Luke's home, or where he was when he wrote Luke/Acts. Paul and his group which included Timothy, Silas, and now Luke then sailed from Troas to Samothrace and on the next day traveled by land to Neapolis and then Philippi. Philippi was the leading city in the Roman Province of Macedonia, and typical of Paul's mission strategy of preaching first in major cities he initially located in Philippi. Paul and his companions remained in Philippi for some time.

Acts 16:11-40: Paul's preaching in Philippi:

Since the events of this narrative are extremely important to our study of Philippians, I am including the full text from Acts regarding Paul's stay in Philippi.

> *11 Setting sail therefore from Troas, we made a direct voyage to Samothrace, and the following day to Ne-apolis, 12 and from there to Philippi, which is the leading city of the district of Macedonia, and a Roman colony. We remained in this city some days; 13 and on the sabbath day we went*

outside the gate to the riverside, where we supposed there was a place of prayer; and we sat down and spoke to the women who had come together. 14 One who heard us was a woman named Lydia, from the city of Thyatira, a seller of purple goods, who was a worshiper of God. The Lord opened her heart to give heed to what was said by Paul. 15 And when she was baptized, with her household, she besought us, saying, "If you have judged me to be faithful to the Lord, come to my house and stay." And she prevailed upon us.

16 As we were going to the place of prayer, we were met by a slave girl who had a spirit of divination and brought her owners much gain by soothsaying. 17 She followed Paul and us, crying, "These men are servants of the Most High God, who proclaim to you the way of salvation." 18 And this she did for many days. But Paul was annoyed, and turned and said to the spirit, "I charge you in the name of Jesus Christ to come out of her." And it came out that very hour.

19 But when her owners saw that their hope of gain was gone, they seized Paul and Silas and dragged them into the market place before the rulers; 20 and when they had brought them to the magistrates they said, "These men are Jews and they are disturbing our city. 21 They advocate customs which it is not lawful for us Romans to accept or practice." 22 The crowd joined in attacking them; and the magistrates tore the garments off them and gave orders to beat them with rods. 23 And when they had inflicted many blows upon them, they threw them into prison, charging the jailer to keep them safely. 24 Having received this charge, he put them into the inner prison and fastened their feet in the stocks.

25 But about midnight Paul and Silas were praying and singing hymns to God, and the prisoners were listening to them, 26 and suddenly there was a great earthquake, so that the foundations of the prison were shaken; and immediately all the doors were opened and every one's fetters were unfastened. 27 When the jailer woke and saw that the prison doors were open, he drew his sword and was about to kill himself, supposing that the prisoners had escaped. 28 But Paul cried with a loud voice, "Do not harm yourself, for we are all here." 29 And he called for lights and rushed in, and

> *trembling with fear he fell down before Paul and Silas, 30 and brought them out and said, "Men, what must I do to be saved?" 31 And they said, "Believe in the Lord Jesus, and you will be saved, you and your household." 32 And they spoke the word of the Lord to him and to all that were in his house. 33 And he took them the same hour of the night, and washed their wounds, and he was baptized at once, with all his family. 34 Then he brought them up into his house, and set food before them; and he rejoiced with all his household that he had believed in God. 35 But when it was day, the magistrates sent the police, saying, "Let those men go." 36 And the jailer reported the words to Paul, saying, "The magistrates have sent to let you go; now therefore come out and go in peace." 37 But Paul said to them, "They have beaten us publicly, uncondemned, men who are Roman citizens, and have thrown us into prison; and do they now cast us out secretly? No! let them come themselves and take us out." 38 The police reported these words to the magistrates, and they were afraid when they heard that they were Roman citizens; 39 so they came and apologized to them. And they took them out and asked them to leave the city. 40 So they went out of the prison, and visited Lydia; and when they had seen the brethren, they exhorted them and departed."*

At this stage of our study as we prepare for our textual examination of Philippians note the important points in this text:

First, Paul found a group of women, presumably mostly Jewish women, meeting for prayer at a river in Philippi. Apparently, there was no Synagogue in Philippi at this time.[4] This practice was is in keeping with Paul's mission strategy of first finding a Synagogue or gathering of Jews where he would have some common ground to his preaching (cf. Acts 13:14; 14:1; 17:1; 18:4; 18:7; 19:8; et al.).

Second, he converted Lydia, a seller of purple dye or cloth, and her household, all of them being baptized. Lydia was obviously a person of some financial means. Lydia is called "a worshipper of God" (σέβομαι, *sébomai*, a worshipper of the divine). This was a technical term used of Gentiles who were attracted to Judaism with its

---

[4] Joseph A. Fitzmyer, *The Acts of the Apostles*, New York: Doubleday, The Anchor Bible, 1998, p. 585.

Law, high ethical code, and monotheism.[5] Lydia invited Paul and his group to stay with her in her house.

Third, Paul had a clash with the pagans of Philippi over a slave girl who had a "spirit of divination" whom Paul challenged. Her owners charged Paul with disturbing the city and creating a turmoil. Paul and Silas were arrested, beaten with rods, and thrown into prison.

Fourth, while singing and praying in prison there was an earthquake which destroyed the gates of the prison. The jailor was afraid and about to kill himself when Paul introduced him to the gospel and taught him about Jesus.

Fifth, the jailor and his household were baptized at once, that "*same hour of the night*" (Acts 16:33).

Sixth, Paul a Roman citizen had been beaten and thrown in prison without trial, contrary to the rights of a Roman citizen. He brought this to the attention of the magistrates and was set free with many apologies from the magistrates.

The Date for Writing Philippians

The best indication of the date or order of writing of the four Prison Epistles was that Philippians was the last of the four epistles Paul wrote from Rome, probably late CE 62 or 63.

At Phil 2:19-24 Paul gave some indication that he might *soon* be released from prison and be able to be with the Philippians.

> *I hope in the Lord Jesus to send Timothy to you soon, so that I may be cheered by news of you.* [20] *I have no one like him, who will be genuinely anxious for your welfare.* [21] *They all look after their own interests, not those of Jesus Christ.* [22] *But Timothy's worth you know, how as a son with a father he has served with me in the gospel.* [23] *I hope therefore to send him just as soon as I see how it will go with me;* [24] *and I trust in the Lord that shortly I myself shall come also.*

There are some recent writers that prefer Ephesus as the place of writing, and if such is the case, then this would affect the date of writing.

---

[5] Fitzmyer, *op. cit.*, p. 520.

Most commentaries on the four prison epistles engage in lengthy discussion of the three major places of writing, Rome, Ephesus, and Caesarea. Nevertheless, we prefer Rome as the place of writing with the CE 62/63 as the date.

Note Fee and Stuart's comments on the dating of Philippians: "probably A.D. 62, almost certainly from Rome."[6]

Note also O'Brien who likewise prefers Rome, with awareness of the uncertainty in the debate.

> Thus, if the letter to the Philippians was written from Rome, it is probably to be placed late in Paul's imprisonment (A.D. 60–62), for the following reasons: (1) it allows time for the situation described in Phil. 1:12–18 to develop; (2) the theme of 'joy' that runs through the letter is set against an impending crisis (1:19–26) that could mark the final climax to his trial, that is, the conclusion to the 'two years' of Acts 28:30; (3) Paul's future plans are conditional on the resolution of that crisis (1:23–25, 27; 2:23–24), and (4) on a late date in the imprisonment it is easier to accommodate the multiple journeys to and from Philippi.[7]

Major Points to Learn from this lesson

1. Philippians was one of four epistles written by Paul from prison in Rome, ca CE 60-63.
2. Philippi was the leading city in the Roman Province of Macedonia, and one of the major cities to the region.
3. On his second mission journey Paul was summoned to Macedonia by a vision of a man from Macedonia calling Paul to "come over and preach the gospel."
4. In Philippi Paul converted Lydia and her household.
5. Paul and Silas ran into trouble with the owner of a slave girl with "a spirit of divination," and the city leaders. He and Silas were abused and beaten and then thrown into prison.
6. As the result of an earthquake that destroyed the gates of the prison, Paul and Silas taught and converted the Philippian

---

[6] Gordon Fee and Douglas Stuart, *How to Read the Bible Book by Book*, Zondervan, Grand Rapids, 2002, p. 353.
[7] O'Brien, *ibid*, p. 26.

jailor and his household, baptizing them immediately the same hour of the night.

Discussion points from this lesson

1. What can we conclude from Paul's vision of the man from Macedonia? How does this fit into the story of Acts and Paul's ministry?
2. Why did Paul go to the river in Philippi to find people praying?
3. Why is Lydia, being a seller of purple from Thyatira, an interesting discussion point regarding the Book of Revelation? Compare Acts 16:14 and Revelation 2:18.
4. Comment on why Paul first instructed the Philippian jailor to believe in Jesus in order to be saved, and then or soon after this, baptized him. Does this mean that the jailor was simply saved by believing in Jesus and then baptized because he was saved? What is going on in this text? Why tell the jailor first to believe in Jesus before baptizing him?

Chapter 2: Paul's Epistolary Style

Understanding the structure of a Pauline epistle, or any epistle, is vital to the interpretation of the epistle. For example, we can partially determine the origin of a letter today merely by examining the date! Compare the dates 12.31.2018 and 31.12.2018. Which one is American, and which is British or European? What does this tell us regarding the author of a letter dated 31.12.2018? Thus, sometimes unnoticed or seemingly insignificant comments help determine an author or the theology of an epistle. This is true of studying New Testament Epistles.

Early in his ministry Paul adapted the typical Graeco/Roman form of letter writing and shaped it into an early Christian Epistolary instructional and exhortative form.[1]

This standard Pauline form of letter writing was structured around four major components: a *Salutation/Prescript*, a *Laudatio*, a *Body*, and a *Conclusion*.[2] These are defined or developed as follows:

1. A *Salutation/Prescript* includes a greeting and salutation in which Paul addressed those to whom he was writing.
2. A *Laudatio* (a praise and prayer section). This section is very important to determining the theology and purpose of the epistle because in this material Paul introduced his *purpose* and the *major theme* of the epistle. The *Laudatio* would generally be in the form of or include a major prayer for the recipients. The *Laudatio* often forms a *Prologue*[3] to the Epistle.
3. The *Body* of the letter which often came in two sections:
    a. *Doctrine/Theology* – which outlines and develops Paul's major premise and argument.
    b. *Paranesis*[4] – in which Paul introduces the practical or ethical implications of the doctrinal material.

---

[1] Cf. Adolf Deissmann, *Light from the Ancient East*, Grand Rapids: Baker Book House, 1965, Leander Keck, *Paul and His Letters*, Fortress Press, 1978, and by Gerald F. Hawthorne, Ralph P. Martin and Daniel G. Reid, *Dictionary of Paul and His Letters: A Compendium of Contemporary Biblical Scholarship*, Downers Grove: InterVarsity Press, 2009.

[2] Some scholars use different yet similar terms to describe these elements of an ancient epistle.

[3] The *Prologue* and *Epilogue* form an *inclusio* which defines the theme or purpose of the body of the Epistle.

[4] *Paranesis* or *paranetic* are technical terms that describe the practical, ethical, and moral implications of the theological or doctrinal material.

4. The *Conclusio* in which Paul summarized his main purpose in writing and mentioned friends and companions with whom the recipients of the letter would be acquainted. The *Conclusio* often forms an *Epilogue* to the Epistle.

Paul's Use of a Prologue and Epilogue as an *Inclusio*

Paul's use of the epistolary *Laudatio* and *Conclusio* follow the traditional Hellenistic style of an epistle in which the writer used the *Laudatio* and *Conclusio* as a *Prologue* and *Epilogue*. The *Laudatio* and *Conclusio* thus serve as an *inclusio*[5] in which the author highlighted, defined, or emphasized the heart or theology of the message.

As we move into this study, we will note the emphasis placed on three principles, *joy* and *rejoicing*, the *role model of the Lord Jesus Christ*, and *the strength of true Christian fellowship* which are matured through the joy of Christian service.

The *Prologue* of Phil 1:3ff and the *Epilogue* of Phil 4:10ff each begin by *emphasizing the joy of Christian fellowship* evident between Paul and the Philippian congregation. Paul thus intended to use his and their relationship as a model to be encouraged within the congregation itself. Although the following comment by Peter O'Brien comes from the *Epilogue* and concluding exhortation of the Epistle, it draws attention to the role played by the *Prologue/Epilogue* and *Laudatio/Conclusio* in this Epistle.

> The apostle now turns to one of the main reasons for his writing the letter, namely, to express his gratitude to the Philippians for their generosity, as evidenced in the gift sent through their messenger, Epaphroditus (2:25–30). Although Paul has already alluded to their kindness (1:3, 5) and written with great affection about Epaphroditus, who in bringing their

---

[5] The term *inclusio* refers to a literary device based on a concentric principle, also known as *bracketing*. The *inclusio* creates boundaries or frame to a literary piece such as an epistle by placing similar material at the beginning and end of the material thus emphasizing or highlighting the meaning or importance of the material between the *inclusios*. The *inclusio* may consist of a word, a phrase, or a paragraph. In the case of a Pauline epistle the inclusios would be the prologue and the epilogue, or the *Laudatio* and *Conclusio*.

gift had almost died (2:25–30), he does not discuss the gift in detail until now. The position of a 'thank you' note at the end of the letter looks like an afterthought, and this, together with the considerable amount of time that has elapsed between the arrival of Epaphroditus with the gift (2:25–30) and the writing of this note, has suggested to many scholars that 4:10–20 are a separate letter written by Paul soon after he received the gift from the Philippians. But this 'drastic, hypothetical solution' is to be rejected ...

As shown above, the introductory thanksgiving paragraph (1:3–11) functions as a prologue setting the tone and anticipating some of the major themes and motifs that bind the whole letter together. This is particularly true in relation to the epilogue (4:10–20), where interconnecting and thematic links with the prologue are made. The two paragraphs form an inclusion,[6] with the affirmation of v. 19 ('My God shall supply all your need ...') and its doxology (v. 20) providing the answer to Paul's intercessory prayer (1:9–11) and the Philippians' other needs as expressed throughout the letter.[7]

Paul's intention was thus to highlight the joy of Christian service in Christ, something which he shared with the Philippians and which he wanted to encourage the Philippians to emulate among themselves.

The Literary Structure of Philippians

1. **Salutation/Prescript**: Phil 1:1-2
2. **Prayer/Laudatio/Prescript**: Phil 1:3-11
3. **Body**: Phil 1:12 – Phil 4:9
   A difficult point in outlining Philippians is that Paul mixes both theology and paranesis as he works through the letter. However, the following is a broad outline of the body of Philippians.
      a. **Theology**: Phil 1:12-30
      b. **Paranesis**: Phil 2:1-Phil 4:9
4. **Conclusion/Epilogue**: Phil 4:10-23

---

[6] As mentioned above in footnote 9 *inclusion/inclusio* is a technical term that functions similar to *parentheses*. The two ends of the *inclusio* primarily define the core of the message between the two *inclusios*.
[7] O'Brien, *ibid.*, pp. 513–514.

The Recipients of the Letter

As we observed above the recipients of the Philippian Epistle were the church in Philippi that Paul, Silas, and Timothy had founded on their second missionary journey ca. CE 49-52, Acts 16:11-40. *It is obvious from the contents of the letter that a close bond of Christian fellowship and friendship existed between the church and Paul.*

The Christians in Philippi were predominantly Gentiles, newly converted to Christianity. However, there were some members who were Jewish and who were experiencing difficulty in a new Christian situation where past Jewish marks of identity such as circumcision were no longer held in high regard. This apparently led to some tension within the congregation.

The Occasion/Purpose of the Letter

According to Paul, Epaphroditus had come from Philippi with news for Paul from the congregation in Philippi and a gift to help with his support. Note Phil 2:25ff and 4:18ff.

> [2:25]*I have thought it necessary to send to you Epaphroditus my brother and fellow worker and fellow soldier, and your messenger and minister to my need,* [26]*for he has been longing for you all, and has been distressed because you heard that he was ill.* [27]*Indeed he was ill, near to death. But God had mercy on him, and not only on him but on me also, lest I should have sorrow upon sorrow.* [28]*I am the more eager to send him, therefore, that you may rejoice at seeing him again, and that I may be less anxious.* [29]*So receive him in the Lord with all joy; and honor such men,* [30]*for he nearly died for the work of Christ, risking his life to complete your service to me.*
>
> [4:18]*I have received full payment, and more; I am filled, having received from Epaphroditus the gifts you sent, a fragrant offering, a sacrifice acceptable and pleasing to God.* [19]*And my God will supply every need of yours according to his riches in glory in Christ Jesus.* [20]*To our God and Father be glory for ever and ever. Amen.*

In his letter Paul was responding with thanksgiving. But Epaphroditus had also brought disturbing news to Paul of developments in the church at Philippi that were creating some tension within the congregation.

There was some false teaching beginning to circulate that was disturbing Epaphroditus and the leadership of the church in Philippi, Phil 1:15ff.

This false teaching had Jewish overtones in which some were claiming that the Christians needed to have the traditional marks of identity such as circumcision in order to be in a right relationship with God, Phil 3:1ff.

There was some inner tension developing between members that was setting up some division within the congregation. This tension arose concerning two ladies in the congregation, Euodia and Syntyche, who for some unidentified reason were not getting along very well, Phil 4:2. Paul encouraged someone, either another fellow-worker whose name might be *Súzugos*,[8] or simply some fellow-worker in general to help the two ladies.

It seems also that tensions with pagan neighbors, a holdover from Paul's opposition of the pagan slave girl with a spirit of divination, was creating pagan Gentile opposition and suffering, possibly even persecution.

The Theology of the Letter

We will note in the next lesson on the *Salutation/Prescript* and the *Prayer/Laudatio/Prologue* (Phil 1:1-11) that Paul stressed the point that *real joy in the Christian life comes through true Christian fellowship and loving service*. To develop this theme Paul used four Christian examples which we will develop in the flow of thought in the epistle: *first* his *own life*, *then* that of *Jesus Christ*, then that of *Timothy*, and *finally* that of *Epaphroditus*.

---

[8] Although the word *súzugos* is a general word for yoke-fellow or fellow-worker some have suggested that this may be the name of someone who Paul knew in Philippi who also knew the two women in question.

In understanding the interweaving of *theology*[9] and *paranesis*[10] in Philippians, which flow together somewhat in the body of the epistle, two salient points must be recognized; *first* Paul seldom if ever makes *theological* statements that stand alone without some practical *paranetic* application; *second*, likewise, he seldom if ever makes *paranetic* arguments without embedding them in major *theological* points that lie at the root of the *paranesis*.

Since Philippi was a major city in the Roman Empire in which a Graeco-Roman culture defined society, three important cultural Graeco-Roman mindsets lie behind much of what Paul was stressing in his Philippian letter.

First, that true friendship (κοινωνία, *koinōnía, fellowship*) played a significant role in the Graeco-Roman culture of the day. True friendships manifest in mutual partnerships were considered admirable characteristics in the Graeco-Roman culture.

Second, most Graeco-Roman philosophers paid considerable attention to moral and ethical encouragement. In the course of his *theological/paranetic* discussion Paul uses himself, Jesus Christ, Timothy, and Epaphroditus as examples of appropriate ethical behavior, especially in their concern for others.

Third, since Philippi was in many ways a Roman colony with high regard for the Imperial cult, it is obvious that Christians would run into some disfavor with the Roman authorities and their pagan neighbors with their claim that Jesus Christ was Lord. Although opposition to this Christian claim had not yet run into Roman opposition as reflected in the Book of Revelation, some local pagan and Roman opposition was present. Paul drew attention to this by demonstrating that in his own case his being a Roman did not necessary impact Christian claims to the Lordship of Christ and the preaching of Christ. Although there could be some theological conflict, politically this need not necessarily be the case. Even in Rome, the seat of the Imperial cult, Paul was later successful in

---

[9] We might briefly define *theology* here as a synonym for *a major doctrinal discussion about God and Jesus Christ who are the foundation and core of all biblical faith and behavior*. We should consider theology then as the doctrinal foundation to Christian behavior. The concept of theology emphasizes that in the doctrinal/theological material Paul establishes how God enters the discussion and frames the behavior anticipated by the readers.

[10] *Paranesis* or *paranetic* statements involve ethical, moral, or practical behavior stimulated by a theological statement.

preaching the Lordship of Jesus and had even penetrated the Imperial Guard in the Praetorium in Rome.

As one reads through the *Laudatio/Prayer* of Philippians, and then the remainder of the epistle, one can hardly miss the *centrality of Christ* in the theological weave of the epistle. Furthermore, two major themes surface in Paul's emphasis on *fellowship* or *genuine partnership* in the gospel and the *genuine joy* inherent in Christians serving one another.

Since the theme of *joy* is mentioned at least five (5) times and *rejoicing* at least nine (9) times, perhaps we should ask why Paul makes such a strong emphasis on these themes! A possible reason was that the Christians in Philippi for several reasons were not enjoying their Christian life as they should which had resulted in Epaphroditus mentioning some of the issues the church was facing. *The joy of Christian service had grown weak due to tensions building within the congregation!*

For this reason, I like to use the term *"blahs"* to describe the spiritual life of the church in Philippi! One dictionary defines the *blahs* as "a feeling of physical uneasiness, general discomfort, or mild depression and malaise." I like to think of *blahs* as one's spiritual batteries running low! Churches and Christians often *plateau* in their Christian life and witness and experience *spiritual lows* or the *blahs*. This seems to be the case in Philippi, hence Paul picks up on this and speaks of *the joy of Christian fellowship and serving one another*.

The central theme, or theology that Paul develops in Philippians is thus that joy in the Christian life comes through loving service to one another in the example of Jesus Christ.

Four important themes to follow in

Philippians

First, the Philippians should not let suffering and hardships discourage them from the power and glory of Christ and the gospel. Phil 1:12, 18; 1:20-23; 1:29; 4:12, 13.

Second, the Philippian Christians are repeatedly *encouraged to rejoice* over the blessings they enjoy in Christ rather than concentrate on the negatives and sufferings they are experiencing. Paul, Christ, Timothy, and Epaphroditus are prime role models of this. Phil 1:4; 2:2; 4:4.

Third, they need to *grow*, *energize*, and *mature* in the salvation that God had begun in them in Christ. Phil 1:6, 9; 1:25; 2:12.

Fourth, God, who began it all for them in Christ, *still desires to work in them and bring them to maturity in Christ*. Phil 1:1:6; 2:12, 13; 4:13, 19.

Major points to learn from this lesson

1. The church in Philippi was established by Paul on his 2nd Missionary Journey ca CE 48/49. Lydia was the first person converted in Philippi followed by her household and the Philippian Jailor and his household.
2. Philippi was a major city in the Roman Province of Macedonia with a strong Imperial cult background.
3. Philippi was a Gentile region with some small Jewish influence – there was no full synagogue present and the Jews met at a river to pray.
4. News had been brought to Paul by Epaphroditus that the church in Philippi was experiencing some difficulties.
5. It seems like church life had bogged down or plateaued with a decline in spiritual joy.
6. Paul stressed that Christian joy comes through loving Christian service after the model of Jesus Christ, and concern for one another.

Discussion points from this lesson

1. What circumstances do we encounter in our lives that cause us to experience the spiritual *blahs*?
2. What can cause a congregation to go into a plateau and experience the spiritual *blahs*?
3. On a personal level what can we do when we feel spiritually down? Where would a good place be for us to begin?
4. Where should our spiritual focus be in our Christian life?

Chapter 3: Salutation and Laudatio Prayer

Phil 1:1-11

The Salutation: Phil 1:1, 2

[1] Paul and Timothy, servants of Christ Jesus,
To all the saints in Christ Jesus who are at Philippi, with the bishops and deacons:
[2] Grace to you and peace from God our Father and the Lord Jesus Christ.

Phil 1:1. Although Silas and Luke had been part of the 2nd missionary journey that brought Paul to Philippi, at this point in his Roman imprisonment only Timothy is mentioned in the salutation. Apparently Silas and Luke had previously left Paul for other mission activities.

In other epistles where Paul's apostleship had been questioned or it had become necessary to remind the churches of the source of his apostleship (1 Corinthians, 2 Corinthians, Galatians, Ephesians, et al.) Paul had stressed that he was an apostle of Jesus Christ, called and commissioned by Jesus Christ. Here with the Philippians this is not mentioned – it simply was not necessary! However, in keeping with the theme of the epistle Paul stresses that he and Timothy were simply *servants of Christ*. Notice the emphasis on *servants*! The word servant is an English translation of the Greek δοῦλος, *doúlos*, which primarily means *a slave or bonded servant*. Paul uses this term widely in his epistles to emphasize the relationship that he and all Christians sustain with Jesus Christ. We are *bonded servants* of Christ.[1] This resonates with the principle Paul states at 1 Cor 6:20, *Do you not know that your body is a temple of the Holy Spirit within you, which you have from God? You are not your own; [20] you were bought with a price. So glorify God in your body*, and 1 Cor 7:33f. *You were bought with a price; do not become slaves of men. [24] So, brethren, in whatever state each was called, there let him remain with God.*

---

[1] Zodhiates, δοῦλος, *doúlos, ibid.*

As was usually the case in ancient letters the writer would identify his readers by name and with some modifier. *First*, Paul addresses the Christians in Philippi as *saints*. The term saint derives from the Greek term ἅγιος, *hágios*. This is a broad term with several facets. Spiros Zodhiates observes regarding the *hágios* word-group:

> "Ἅγιος hágios ... from hágos (referring to) any matter of religious awe, expiation, sacrifice. Holy, set apart, sanctified, consecrated, saint ... Its fundamental idea is separation, consecration, devotion to the service of Deity, sharing in God's purity and abstaining from earth's defilement ... Consecrated, devoted, sacred, holy, meaning set apart from a common to a sacred use; spoken of places, temples, cities, the priesthood, men [2]

Hawthorne and Martin offer an extensive discussion of this significant term providing an excellent definition of the word *hágios* from which I have extracted the following:

> Πᾶσιν τοῖς ἁγίοις ἐν Χριστῷ Ἰησοῦ, "to all God's people incorporate in Christ Jesus." Paul rarely uses the all-inclusive word πᾶς, "all," to address the readers of his letters (only in Rom 1:7 and Phil 1:1). He does so here, one suspects, as a watchword ... because there was dissension in Philippi and not everyone was convinced that he or she was included in the apostle's concern. The startling frequency of the expression "all of you" with which Paul continually addresses the Philippian Christians (Phil 1:4, 7 [2x], 8, 25; 2:17, 26; cf. 4:21, 23mg) indicates that he is subtly but forcefully calling them to unity, assuring them all of his love and prayers, and telling them that he was writing not only to those who continually brought him joy (4:1), but also to those whose actions tended to fracture the church (4:2–3). None was excluded.
>
> Ἅγιοι is often translated "saints." With this word Paul regularly addresses the Christians to whom he is writing, to draw attention not primarily to the ethical character of their lives (i.e., "saintly," "pious") but to their special relationship to God; not here to their moral qualities, as if there were no longer any sinners at Philippi, but to the new ground of their existence (Gnilka).

---

[2] Zodhiates, ἅγιος *hágios, op. cit.*

Ἅγιος, "holy," has a long history of meaning. Originally it was applied only to the gods as beings who commanded religious awe (ἅγιος) or were worthy of veneration (ἄζεσθαι, "to stand in awe of"). Later it was also applied to persons and things, because of their special relation to the gods. By virtue of this special relationship, therefore, they were separated from the profane world about them so as to be ceremonially pure enough to perform special service for, or be used in special rites pertaining to, the worship of these gods.

In the LXX ἅγιος is used chiefly to translate קדש qōdeš, a Hebrew word with essentially the same meanings as the Greek word … (ἅγιος) Yahweh makes a covenant with Israel, and as a result Israel is called holy, God's elect people, a nation separated from all the other nations of the world (Exod 19:5–6; Lev 11:44–45). Israel was holy because of God's gracious choice (cf. Asting, Heiligkeit, who writes: the holy ones are such "not only as living for a while in the evil world and not belonging to that world, but as elect children of God and members of the coming kingdom" … Therefore, to translate ἅγιοι as "God's people," rather than the traditional and often misunderstood "saints," is fully justified, capturing better the root meaning of the word and showing more clearly that Paul viewed the members of the Christian church as the New Israel, the new community separated and dedicated to God, the eschatological people, the people of the end time, to whom God would make good his promises …[3]

In summary then, a *saint* is God's person, *cleansed from the world of sin, and dedicated and consecrated to God and his service.*

The verb form of this word, ἁγιάζω, *hagiázō* is found in an interesting but meaningful manner in 2 Tim 2:21 which expresses many of the same concerns of Christian service. For emphasis, I have set the word **consecrated** in the following text in bold. *Consecrated* is translated from the Greek ἡγιασμένον, which is a perfect participle, *hēgiasmenon, of the Greek verb* ἁγιάζω, *hagiázō,*[4] which is often translated as *to sanctify or cleanse.* Note 2 Tim 2:21:

---

[3] Hawthorne, G. F., *ibid*, pp. 6–7.
[4] Zodhiates, ἁγιάζω, *hagiázō, ibid.,* "to make holy, sanctify, to consecrate, devote, set apart from a common to a sacred use since in the Jewish ritual, this was one great object of the purifications."

> [20] *In a great house there are not only vessels of gold and silver but also of wood and earthenware, and some for noble use, some for ignoble.* [21] *If any one purifies himself from what is ignoble, then he will be a vessel for noble use,* **consecrated** *and useful to the master of the house, ready for any good work.* [22] *So shun youthful passions and aim at righteousness, faith, love, and peace, along with those who call upon the Lord from a pure heart.* [23] *Have nothing to do with stupid, senseless controversies; you know that they breed quarrels.* [24] *And the Lord's servant must not be quarrelsome but kindly to everyone, an apt teacher, forbearing,* [25] *correcting his opponents with gentleness.*

The saint is thus God's person in Christ who has been cleansed by the blood of Christ and is now dedicated or consecrated to Christ and Christian service. Paul intends the Christians in Philippi, *all of them*, to understand that they are God's people, *dedicated to Christian service*. This includes all the members, especially as he mentions by ministry *the bishops and the deacons in his salutation*!

It is interesting and informative that it is here and only here in any of his epistles that Paul addresses the letter not only to the church but to the *bishops and deacons*! The bishops, who are also designated in the New Testament as elders or shepherds are the congregational leaders with a specific ministry of leading the congregation by example and service. Cf Acts 20:28; 1 Pet 5:1-3 where the three leadership terms, *elders, bishops, shepherds* are used to describe the same persons. Thus the *elders* who are *shepherds* are also *overseers* who have several ministries or "hats" involved in leading, teaching, shepherding, and caring for the "flock" or congregation.

It is not surprising that Paul addresses both the *bishops* (the Greek term for bishop is ἐπισκόποι, *epískopoi, an overseer who looks over and after a congregation*) and *deacons* (the Greek term is διακόνοι, *diákonoi*, who are *special servants whose ministry is to serve*). It was their responsibility to be examples of *dedicated* and *consecrated servants* of God and Christ in the life of the congregation. Somehow for some reason in Paul's mind they must have been slacking in their care of the congregation and leadership in Christian service, hence, he mentions them by "name"!

Thus, the message of being a *consecrated servant* had a triple impact! It was addressed to the *overseers* of the congregation who had the ministry of *looking out over* and *for* the congregation, and to the deacons as *special servants* whose ministry was to be *dedicated* servants, and to the *saints* who had been sanctified for the service God. The message was especially relevant for everyone in the congregation!

It is evident from his greeting to the congregation that Paul had dedicated Christian service on his mind!

Phil 1:2. The expression *"Grace to you and peace"* was in the typical Pauline epistolary greeting tradition. This greeting was intended not only as a greeting but also as a prayer that the Philippians would continue to enjoy the blessings of God's gracious favor.

Loh and Nida agree that the greeting in fact is a blessing and a prayer for the Philippians:

> This type of blessing or benediction must be identified in some languages as a kind of prayer, and so must be introduced by a verb specifically indicating prayer, for example, "I pray that God our Father and the Lord Jesus Christ will give you grace and peace."[5]

However, in Paul's salutation the verb "I pray..." is implied, not mentioned. The sense of a continuation of blessing is also implied.

Melick likewise expresses the theological nature of Paul's salutation as a prayer:

> The specific greeting, "grace and peace," adds to the normal epistolary introductions. Since grace always reminded Paul of God's grace in Christ, no doubt this word conveys full Christian meaning. It means "may God's grace be with you." The fact that Paul placed it before "peace" may indicate further his theological orientation that grace provided for and secured peace. "Peace" no doubt conveyed Paul's Hebrew background and the typical greeting "shalom." It had a full sense of "may all things be well with you." Both words as used by Paul imply a petition as well as a greeting.[6]

Hawthorne and Martin comment on this:

---

[5] Loh, I-J., & Nida, E. A. *A Handbook on Paul's Letter to the Philippians*, New York: United Bible Societies, 1995, p. 8.

[6] Melick, R. R. *Philippians, Colossians, Philemon*, Nashville: Broadman & Holman Publishers, 1991, p. 51.

"Χάρις ὑμῖν καὶ εἰρήνη, "grace to you and peace." The salutation of the letter form current in the Greco-Roman world of Paul's day invariably concluded with the word χαίρειν, "greetings," or the phrases πλεῖστα χαίρειν or πολλὰ χαίρειν, "abundant greetings" ... Paul follows this form. But in a clever play on the sound of the standardized and expected χαίρειν [chairein], "greetings," he deliberately substitutes χάρις [charis], "grace" ... This latter word is a definitely Christian word, used 155 times in the NT, and a key term in Paul's letters, used by him approximately 100 times. Through it he conveys to his readers more than his own personal greetings. He stresses each time the idea of the free, spontaneous, unmerited favor of God. God is now "for them," having acted in grace toward them on the basis of the death of Christ ... But Paul changes the standardized Greco-Roman formula of salutation still further. Correspondence of that period generally limited the greeting to a single word (χαίρειν) with its appropriate modifiers. Paul, however, not only replaces χαίρειν, "greetings," with χάρις, "grace," but regularly adds to it the word εἰρήνη, "peace." Χάρις καὶ εἰρήνη, "grace and peace," then, is his most frequently used formula of greeting (Rom 1:7; 1 Cor 1:3; 2 Cor 1:2; Gal 1:3; Eph 1:2; Phil 1:2; Col 1:2; 1 Thess 1:1; 2 Thess 1:2; Phlm 3; but cf. 1 Tim 1:2; Titus 1:2; many MSS of Titus 1:4 and 2 John 3, where the greeting χάρις, ἔλεος, εἰρήνη, "grace, mercy, and peace," appears). He thus combines Western and Eastern salutations in his new formula, "peace" being the standard Jewish or oriental form of greeting ... But once again the commonplace is used in an uncommon way—an ordinary salutation is elevated into a benediction ..., for εἰρήνη, "peace," like the word grace, is linked with the activity of God. As a result, "peace" comes to mean in Paul "harmony," "tranquility," "wholeness," "well-being," "salvation" of the total person, reconciliation of persons and societies to God as well as to one another—peace at the deepest level. The whole greeting, χάρις καὶ εἰρήνη, "grace and peace," therefore, states that the OT dream for the future is being fulfilled ... and, therefore, it "becomes an epitome of all that is central and essential in the Christian religion..."[7]

Regarding *grace*, Zodhiates observes:

> "Χάρις cháris... to rejoice. Grace, particularly that which causes joy, pleasure, gratification, favor, acceptance, for a kindness granted or desired, a benefit, thanks, gratitude. A favor done without expectation of return; the absolutely free expression of the loving kindness of God to men finding its only motive in the bounty and benevolence of the Giver; unearned and unmerited favor. Cháris stands in direct antithesis to érga ... works, the two being mutually exclusive. God's grace affects man's sinfulness and not only forgives the repentant sinner but brings joy and thankfulness to him. It changes the individual to a new creature without destroying his individuality."[8]

Paul adds to this prayer for grace an ingredient of *the peace that only God can provide through Jesus Christ*. The Greek word εἰρήνη, *eirēnē* is parallel or similar to the Hebrew word *shalom* which implies a spiritual blessing of spiritual peace from God and with God. Again Zodhiates has some interesting thoughts to add to this:

> "In the OT the equivalent word, shalom ... meant wholeness, soundness, hence health, well–being, prosperity; more particularly, peace as opposed to war ... or concord as opposed to strife ... God is said to be a God of peace, not as one who needs peace, but one who dispenses peace. He expects peace of His people, meaning the absence of confusion ... He rewards those who practice this peace ... Peace is a blessing of which God alone is the author..."[9]

To clarify the matter Paul adds that this grace and peace, that is spiritual favor and tranquility comes, "from God our Father and the Lord Jesus Christ." *We enjoy grace and peace by being in a right relationship with God through Jesus Christ.*

This theologically loaded greeting/prayer leads naturally into the laudatory prayer that follows. In this laudatio prayer we find all of the theological concerns Paul had for the Philippians.

---

[7] Hawthorne, G. F. and Ralph P. Martin, *Philippians*, pp. 12–13. Emphasis mine, IAF.
[8] Zodhiates, S. *ibid.*
[9] Zodhiates, S. *op. cit.* Emphasis mine, IAF.

The Laudatio/Prayer/Prologue: Phil 1:3-11

"³I thank my God in all my remembrance of you, always in every prayer of mine for you all making my prayer with joy, ⁵thankful for your partnership in the gospel from the first day until now. ⁶And I am sure that he who began a good work in you will bring it to completion at the day of Jesus Christ. ⁷It is right for me to feel thus about you all, because I hold you in my heart, for you are all partakers with me of grace, both in my imprisonment and in the defense and confirmation of the gospel. ⁸For God is my witness, how I yearn for you all with the affection of Christ Jesus. ⁹And it is my prayer that your love may abound more and more, with knowledge and all discernment, ¹⁰so that you may approve what is excellent, and may be pure and blameless for the day of Christ, ¹¹filled with the fruits of righteousness which come through Jesus Christ, to the glory and praise of God."

Certain theological themes surface from this *Laudatio/Prayer*.

Phil 1:3-11. As in most of his introductory *laudatios* Paul began by praising the Christians, giving thanks for them and his relationship with them. Inter-Christian relationships becomes a significant theme Paul develops in the Epistle.

First, as usual, Paul's pastoral concern for the congregations he established or with whom he worked is clearly manifest in *the repeated mention of payer* in his greetings. He prayed regularly for them. This is clear here to the Philippians, as it was in the leading statements of his epistles to several other congregations. Cf 1 Cor 1:4; Col 1:3; II Tim 1:3; 1 Thess 1:2; II Thess 1:3; Philemon 1:3.

Second, Paul emphasizes his concern for the Philippians maintaining a continuing and maturing partnership in the gospel. Mention of the term gospel stresses that the purpose of the gospel was to unite Christians with God and Christ and with one another. Note Paul's concern in Ephesians, Galatians, and Romans for Jews and Gentiles getting along with one another in Christ. Now in Philippi it was necessary for Paul to remind the Philippians what the purpose of the gospel was to reconcile all to God and Christ and to one another in Christ and peace.

D. A. Carson and others draw attention to the importance of understanding the purpose and power of the term gospel:

> Both from Paul's example and from that of the Philippians, then, *we must learn this first point: the fellowship of the gospel, the partnership of the gospel, must be put at the center of our relationships with other believers.* That is the burden of these opening verses. Paul does not commend them for the fine times they had shared watching games in the arena. He doesn't mention their literature discussion groups or the excellent meals they had, although undoubtedly, they had enjoyed some fine times together. What lies at the center of all his ties with them, doubtless including meals and discussion, is this passion for the gospel, this partnership in the gospel.[10]
>
> … *But what must tie us together as Christians is this passion for the gospel*, this fellowship in the gospel. On the face of it, nothing else is strong enough to hold together the extraordinary diversity of people who constitute many churches: men and women, young and old, blue collar and white, healthy and ill, fit and flabby, different races, different incomes, different levels of education, different personalities. *What holds us together? It is the gospel, the good news that in Jesus, God himself has reconciled us to himself.* This brings about a precious God-centeredness that we share with other believers.[11]

Third, Paul draws attention to *God who continues to work* in the lives of the Philippians through Jesus Christ.

Fourth, Paul's deep, heart-felt awareness of God's working of grace in their lives is evident in his prayer for the Philippians.

Fifth, one cannot miss Paul's great affection for the Philippians.

Sixth, Paul's prayer that their *love may continue to grow but with discernment* is clearly evident in his concern for some broken relationships in the congregation as in the case of Euodia and Syntyche.

Seventh, Paul prays that they may approve what is *excellent* in their lives in keeping with a Graeco-Roman concern for *ethical* excellence. The expression *may approve what is excellent* is an

---

[10] Carson, D. A., *Basics for Believers: An Exposition of Philippians*, Grand Rapids: Baker Publishing, 1996. kindle locations 147-151.
[11] Carson, *op. cit.* kindle locations 154-158.

interesting translation of the Greek δοκιμάζω, *dokimázō* which primarily means *to test, be approved, to prove, to discern, to distinguish*. It has the notion of proving whether a thing is ethically worthy or not.[12]

Carson expresses this well. Paul's prayer is that the Philippians may discern what is the best behavior, notably in regard to their personal relations:

> ... for Paul this prayer has a further end in view. He lifts these petitions to God, he tells the Philippians, "so that you may be able to discern what is best and may be pure and blameless until the day of Christ" (1:10). Clearly, Paul does not want the Philippian believers to be satisfied with mediocrity. He cannot be satisfied, in a fallen world, with the status quo. He wants these believers to move on, to become more and more discerning, proving in their own experience "what is best." He wants them to pursue what is best in the knowledge of God, what is best in their relationships with other believers, what is best in joyful obedience.[13]

Eighth, Paul prays that they may be filled with the fruits of *a right relationship with God and Jesus*. This is similar to Paul's teaching at Gal 5:16ff where being led by the Spirit and manifesting the fruits of the Spirit in love, joy, peace, patience, kindness, goodness, faithfulness and gentleness is a sign of a right relationship with God.

Ninth, Paul is concerned that the Philippians' lives would be lived to the glory of God. In Eph 1:3-14 Paul explained that God had called Christians in Christ so that they should live for the praise of his glory.

The Conclusion of the Laudatio

The *Laudatio/Prayer* of Philippians resonates with emphasis on Christian *partnership, concern for one another, God's gracious working in their lives*, and *a concern for mature Christ-like living to the praise of the glory of God*. All of this leads us to realize that Paul was aware of a breach in congregation relations, and that he was

---

[12] Zodhiates, δοκιμάζω, *dokimázō, ibid*.
[13] Carson, *ibid*. kindle locations 187-192.

concerned with restoring sincere relationships within the Philippian congregation. He realized how they related to one another would reflect on God's glory in that it was God who had worked in their lives through the gospel story and was still working in their lives through Jesus Christ. Note how Paul later picks up the theme of God working in their lives at Phil 2:12-16:

> *^{12}Therefore, my beloved, as you have always obeyed, so now, not only as in my presence but much more in my absence, work out your own salvation with fear and trembling; ^{13}for God is at work in you, both to will and to work for his good pleasure.*
>
> *^{14}Do all things without grumbling or questioning, ^{15}that you may be blameless and innocent, children of God without blemish in the midst of a crooked and perverse generation, among whom you shine as lights in the world, ^{16}holding fast the word of life, so that in the day of Christ I may be proud that I did not run in vain or labor in vain.*

Major points to learn from this lesson

1. Note well the epistolary ingredients and make-up of Paul's epistles which include the salutation/prescript and the laudatio/prayer which form a prologue to the epistle. Note also that the body of the epistle is a mixture of theological/paranetic material. The conclusio also functions as an epilogue to the epistle.
2. Note Paul's obvious concern for mutual Christian fellowship and service both within the congregation and between the congregation and himself.
3. Pay attention to the fact that Paul stresses that their God who had begun their salvation in Christ, the gospel story, wished to continue working with them to fulfil his working and bring their salvation and faith to maturity.

Discussion points from this lesson

1. Discuss the meaning of being a saint and its implications for Christian service. Remember 2 Tim 2:21!
2. Why did Paul include the bishops and deacons in his salutation?

3. What is the character of the Christian greeting *"grace and peace"*?
4. What practical thoughts can you glean and learn from Paul's Salutation and Laudatio? Discuss how these can and should play out in your own life. Think in terms of your relationship with other Christians and the congregation as a whole.

Chapter 4: Paul's Present Circumstances and a Suitable Philippian Response

Phil 1:12-26

The Theological Model: Paul's Present Circumstances: Phil 1:12-26

¹²I want you to know, brethren, that what has happened to me has really served to advance the gospel, ¹³so that it has become known throughout the whole praetorian guard and to all the rest that my imprisonment is for Christ; ¹⁴and most of the brethren have been made confident in the Lord because of my imprisonment, and are much more bold to speak the word of God without fear.

¹⁵Some indeed preach Christ from envy and rivalry, but others from good will. ¹⁶The latter do it out of love, knowing that I am put here for the defense of the gospel; ¹⁷the former proclaim Christ out of partisanship, not sincerely but thinking to afflict me in my imprisonment. ¹⁸What then? Only that in every way, whether in pretense or in truth, Christ is proclaimed; and in that I rejoice.

¹⁹Yes, and I shall rejoice. For I know that through your prayers and the help of the Spirit of Jesus Christ this will turn out for my deliverance, ²⁰as it is my eager expectation and hope that I shall not be at all ashamed, but that with full courage now as always Christ will be honored in my body, whether by life or by death. ²¹For to me to live is Christ, and to die is gain. ²²If it is to be life in the flesh, that means fruitful labor for me. Yet which I shall choose I cannot tell. ²³I am hard pressed between the two. My desire is to depart and be with Christ, for that is far better. ²⁴But to remain in the flesh is more necessary on your account. ²⁵Convinced of this, I know that I shall remain and continue with you all, for your progress and joy in the faith, ²⁶so that in me you may have ample cause to glory in Christ Jesus, because of my coming to you again.

Paul clearly wants the Philippians to know that life's difficulties, including opposition from either Roman or Pagan opposition, or from false teachers, should not detract from the always present and urgent need to preach and witness to the gospel.

Phil 1:12. Note his opening comment; *I want you to know, brethren, that what has happened to me has really served to advance the gospel* ... Even while in house arrest in Rome Paul has been able to reach into the highly select Roman Praetorian Guard. The Praetorian Guard were a select group of highly trained soldiers for the protection of the Emperor or Imperial Governors of the Roman world. How Paul managed to penetrate this guard is not the point! Paul's point was that he had used his situation and his difficult circumstances to share the gospel with others, even his pagan prison guards.

Phil 1:14-18. Thus, Paul explained how in Rome most of the brethren have been made confident in the Lord because of his imprisonment and are much more bold to speak the word of God without fear. Paul wanted the Philippians to not be discouraged by his difficult circumstances and certainly not to permit their own difficulties to negate their witness or service to one another in love.

Paul was aware that many would preach the gospel for negative means, possibly trying to discredit him. It seems apparent from the context of his comment and other matters relating to circumcision that Paul was aware that certain Jewish Christians did not like his message of a righteous relationship with God through grace and faith in Jesus and not through keeping the Law of Moses. Nevertheless, that Christ was preached, even if in poor spirit, was a plus for the gospel of Christ, and Paul rejoiced even in this opposition. Note his comment at Phil 1:15:

> [15]*Some indeed preach Christ from envy and rivalry, but others from good will.* [16]*The latter do it out of love, knowing that I am put here for the defense of the gospel;* [17]*the former proclaim Christ out of partisanship, not sincerely but thinking to afflict me in my imprisonment.* [18]*What then? Only that in every way, whether in pretense or in truth, Christ is proclaimed; and in that I rejoice.*

Phil 1:19. Paul wrote *Yes, and I shall rejoice. For I know that through your prayers and the help of the Spirit of Jesus Christ this will turn out for my deliverance.*

Note the double reference to rejoice, *and in that I rejoice.*

Yes, and I shall rejoice. Joy and *rejoice* are key ingredients in Paul's message to Philippians, a congregation experiencing the blahs!

This possibly indicates that Paul expected his imminent release from Roman incarceration or house arrest. It has been suggested by some that Roman jurisprudence required that one's accusers needed to appear before the courts within two years of accusation to bring official charges against the person accused.[1] As an educated Roman citizen Paul would have been keenly aware of this. His Jewish accusers in Jerusalem, thinking they had finally got rid of Paul, thought that leaving him in Rome would discourage him. They did not make the journey to Rome to officially accuse Paul.

Paul apparently expected to shortly be released. He wanted the Philippians to know, however, that even the difficulty of being a prisoner in Rome had not discouraged him to where he had quit his gospel message of serving. He had rented a house and used it as a base for his ministry.

Phil 1:20-26. This pericope is one of the truly amazing and striking passages in Paul's many great messages! Serving for and in Christ was a profoundly important part of Paul's life.

> *... but that with full courage now as always* <u>*Christ will be honored in my body, whether by life or by death.* [21] *For to me to live is Christ, and to die is gain*</u>. [22] *If it is to be life in the flesh, that means fruitful labor for me. Yet which I shall choose I cannot tell.* [23] *I am hard pressed between the two. My desire is to depart and be with Christ, for that is far better.* [24] *But to remain in the flesh is more necessary on your account.* [25] *Convinced of this, I know that I shall remain and continue with you all, for your progress and joy in the faith,* [26] *so that in me you may have ample cause to glory in Christ Jesus, because of my coming to you again.*

Paul was clearly aware that his own example of living and dying for Christ would encourage the Philippians to see how their own lives of Christian service for Christ would impact the power of the gospel.

---

[1] Cf. the discussion of this in Joseph A. Fitzmyer, *The Acts of the Apostles*, New York: Doubleday, The Anchor Bible, 1998, pp.796f, F. F. Bruce, *The Book of Acts*, Grand Rapids: Wm. B. Eerdmans, 1954, pp. 534f. Some scholars have questioned the point of a 2-year imprisonment waiting for the Jews to arrive in Rome. But there must have been some reason for Paul to delay his stay in Rome for 2 years.

Phil 1:21. Paul's statement at Phil 1:21, *for to me to live is Christ and to die is gain* is so important for understanding Paul's life and the central message of the Philippian epistle that I have in the above text emphasized it in bold font! Paul states in amazing clarity the central and driving influence and purpose of his life. It was ***first and foremost to live and to die for Christ***! Paul knew that he owed everything in his life to God's grace in revealing Christ to him.

From Paul's road to Damascus experience on throughout his life his purpose became simply to live and die for Christ. His appreciation for God's grace became the primary motivation for his life and ministry.

Note how Paul's awareness of God's grace motivated him in his ministry and Christian witness,1 Cor 15:9ff and Rom 1:14:

> 1 Cor 15:9. *For I am the least of the apostles, unfit to be called an apostle, because I persecuted the church of God. ^{10}But by the grace of God I am what I am, and his grace toward me was not in vain. On the contrary, I worked harder than any of them, though it was not I, but the grace of God which is with me. ^{11}Whether then it was I or they, so we preach and so you believed.*
>
> Rom 1:13. *I want you to know, brethren, that I have often intended to come to you (but thus far have been prevented), in order that I may reap some harvest among you as well as among the rest of the Gentiles. ^{14}I am under obligation both to Greeks and to barbarians, both to the wise and to the foolish: ^{15}So I am eager to preach the gospel to you also who are in Rome.*

Paul's desire to be a servant of Christ, motivated by God's grace, was demonstrated in his sincere concern for the Philippians, especially regarding their interpersonal relationships and congregational life. Placing a sincere interest in others and their spiritual welfare before self obviously was a major theme of his epistle to the Philippians. Discussing his theme becomes the *paranetic*[2] or practical thrust of the following paragraphs of the body of the epistle beginning at Phil 2:1.

---

[2] For convenience we need to have another look at the word *paranetic*! We referenced this in the introduction to this study. *Paranesis* or *paranetic* are technical terms that describe the practical, ethical, moral implications of the theological or doctrinal material.

The Paranesis: A Desired Philippian Response: Phil 1:27-30

^{27} Only let your manner of life be worthy of the gospel of Christ, so that whether I come and see you or am absent, I may hear of you that you stand firm in one spirit, with one mind striving side by side for the faith of the gospel, ^{28} and not frightened in anything by your opponents. This is a clear omen to them of their destruction, but of your salvation, and that from God. ^{29} For it has been granted to you that for the sake of Christ you should not only believe in him but also suffer for his sake, ^{30} engaged in the same conflict which you saw and now hear to be mine.

Phil 1:27. Paul's mention of *your opponents* and his encouragement to live *worthily of the gospel of Christ* addressed one of the issues troubling the Christians. Paul was concerned that the Philippians should not be discouraged by the presence of distractors that preached a different gospel they had accepted. Such opposition was to be expected

Phil 1:28. Paul was concerned that the Philippians would not be frightened by the teaching of the false teachers. Their teaching a different gospel was a sure sign of their ultimate judgment by God. At the time of his writing Philippians and the Prison Epistles most Christians would have been aware of Paul's letter to the Galatians and his dramatic condemnation of false teachers, Gal 1:6-11:

> *I am astonished that you are so quickly deserting him who called you in the grace of Christ and turning to a different gospel— ^{7} not that there is another gospel, but there are some who trouble you and want to pervert the gospel of Christ. ^{8} But even if we, or an angel from heaven, should preach to you a gospel contrary to that which we preached to you, let him be accursed. ^{9} As we have said before, so now I say again, If any one is preaching to you a gospel contrary to that which you received, let him be accursed.*

> [10] *Am I now seeking the favor of men, or of God? Or am I trying to please men? If I were still pleasing men, I should not be a servant of Christ.*
> [11] *For I would have you know, brethren, that the gospel which was preached by me is not man's gospel.*

I will comment below on Paul's understanding of the term *gospel*.

The presence of false teachers was a major distraction in the early church, just as it has continued through the ages. For whatever reason, sometimes in defense of their own doctrines, or in defense of their own importance, false teachers were a constant threat to the young new Christian congregations. The New Testament writings are replete with warnings against such challenges to the faith. Several passages make this point clearly. The Apostle John saw this burgeoning threat. Cf. 1 John 4:1ff:

> *Beloved, do not believe every spirit, but test the spirits to see whether they are of God; for many false prophets have gone out into the world.* [2] *By this you know the Spirit of God: every spirit which confesses that Jesus Christ has come in the flesh is of God,* [3] *and every spirit which does not confess Jesus is not of God. This is the spirit of antichrist, of which you heard that it was coming, and now it is in the world already.* [4] *Little children, you are of God, and have overcome them; for he who is in you is greater than he who is in the world.*

Likewise, Paul warned Timothy and the Ephesian church at 1 Tim 4:1ff:

> *Now the Spirit expressly says that in later times some will depart from the faith by giving heed to deceitful spirits and doctrines of demons,* [2] *through the pretensions of liars whose consciences are seared,* [3] *who forbid marriage and enjoin abstinence from foods which God created to be received with thanksgiving by those who believe and know the truth.*

Again, at Titus 1:10, Paul wrote regarding the need for faithful elders/bishops who would protect the church:

> *For there are many insubordinate men, empty talkers and deceivers, especially the circumcision party;* [11] *they must be silenced, since they are upsetting whole families by teaching for base gain what they have no right to teach.* [12] *One of themselves, a prophet of their own, said, "Cretans are always*

liars, evil beasts, lazy gluttons." ^{13} This testimony is true. Therefore rebuke them sharply, that they may be sound in the faith, ^{14} instead of giving heed to Jewish myths or to commands of men who reject the truth. ^{15} To the pure all things are pure, but to the corrupt and unbelieving nothing is pure; their very minds and consciences are corrupted. ^{16} They profess to know God, but they deny him by their deeds; they are detestable, disobedient, unfit for any good deed.

Phil 1:27-30. Paul expressed the desire to know that whether he was present or absent he wanted to hear reports of the Philippians faithfulness to Christ and the gospel message. Stressing the urgency of his concern, notice Paul's final comment at Phil 1: 29, 30 that, *"you should not only believe in him but also suffer for his sake, ^{30} engaged in the same conflict which you saw and now hear to be mine."* Interestingly, the verb *believe* is in the present infinitive tense, πιστεύειν, *pisteuein*, implying that the Philippians had *continued to believe in him* as they had done in the past.

Paul encouraged the Philippians to draw on his own experience and response, of which they were obviously aware, in difficult times. They could surely recall his own misfortune, beatings, and imprisonment in Philippi as recorded in Acts 16!

However, his exhortation went deeper than that, *notably to honoring the gospel of Christ!* They needed to stand fast *in one spirit with one mind, side by side* with Paul since they and Paul were *engaged in the same battle. The exhortation was to maintain the harmony and unity of the congregation as the one body of Christ, standing side by side in the battle for Christ and the gospel.* Notice the similarity to Eph 4:1-3! The Philippians like the Ephesians were to lead a life worthy of their calling and worthy of the gospel of Christ. Note Eph 4:1,

I, therefore, a prisoner for the Lord, beg you to lead a life worthy of the calling to which you have been called, ^{2} with all lowliness and meekness, with patience, forbearing one another in love, ^{3} eager to maintain the unity of the Spirit in the bond of peace ...

A major theme, possibly a central ingredient of Paul's ministry, was the gospel of Christ, that is concerning Christ. The emphasis in the preaching of Christ was his death, burial, resurrection and appearance before many. Note 1 Cor 15:1-8. For emphasis I have set certain thoughts in bold in the following text:

> *Now I would remind you, brethren, <u>in what terms I preached to you the gospel</u>, which you received, in which you stand, ² **by which you are saved**, if you hold it fast—unless you believed in vain.*
>
> *³ For I delivered to you as <u>of first importance what I also received, that Christ died for our sins in accordance with the scriptures, ⁴ that he was buried, that he was raised on the third day in accordance with the scriptures, ⁵ and that he appeared to Cephas, then to the twelve.</u> ⁶ Then he appeared to more than five hundred brethren at one time, most of whom are still alive, though some have fallen asleep. ⁷ Then he appeared to James, then to all the apostles. ⁸ <u>Last of all, as to one untimely born, he appeared also to me</u>.*

The gospel in Paul's mind was simply that Jesus had died on the cross, had been buried, had risen from the dead and was alive especially in the lives of the disciples. *Nothing less, and nothing more!*

Notice also Paul's statement on the wisdom of God revealed in the death, burial, and resurrection of Christ at 1 Cor 1:17ff:

> *¹⁷ For Christ did not send me to baptize but to preach the gospel, and not with eloquent wisdom, lest the cross of Christ be emptied of its power.*
>
> *¹⁸ For the word of the cross is folly to those who are perishing, but to us who are being saved it is the power of God. ¹⁹ For it is written,*
>
> *"I will destroy the wisdom of the wise,*
> *and the cleverness of the clever I will thwart."*
>
> *²⁰ Where is the wise man? Where is the scribe? Where is the debater of this age? Has not God made foolish the wisdom of the world? ²¹ For since, in the wisdom of God, the world did not know God through wisdom, it pleased God through the folly of what we preach to save those who believe. ²² For Jews demand signs and Greeks seek wisdom, ²³ but we preach Christ crucified, a stumbling block to Jews and folly to Gentiles, ²⁴ but to those who are called, both Jews and Greeks, Christ the power of God and the wisdom of God. ²⁵ For the*

> *foolishness of God is wiser than men, and the weakness of God is stronger than men.*

This is a remarkable statement! Paul was not denying the importance of baptism! He was stressing that without the gospel, the death, burial, and resurrection of Jesus—even baptism—would be only the wisdom of man!

One of the primary reasons for Paul's form, even intense emphasis on the nature of the gospel of Christ was the insistence by certain Jews, whether Christian Jews or non-Christian Jews, of binding the Law of Moses on Christians in addition to faith in Jesus, possibly even denial of the death and resurrection of Jesus. Paul would have nothing of this. The *gospel* (good news) of the death and resurrection of Jesus was all that was needed for salvation and a right relationship with God.

Two texts stress this gospel. First, one emphasizing the all sufficiency of Christ, Col 1:15-23:

> *He is the image of the invisible God, the first-born of all creation; ^{16} for in him all things were created, in heaven and on earth, visible and invisible, whether thrones or dominions or principalities or authorities—all things were created through him and for him. ^{17} He is before all things, and in him all things hold together. ^{18} He is the head of the body, the church; he is the beginning, the first-born from the dead, that in everything he might be pre-eminent. ^{19} For in him all the fulness of God was pleased to dwell, ^{20} and through him to reconcile to himself all things, whether on earth or in heaven, making peace by the blood of his cross.*
>
> *^{21} And you, who once were estranged and hostile in mind, doing evil deeds, ^{22} he has now reconciled in his body of flesh by his death, in order to present you holy and blameless and irreproachable before him, ^{23} provided that you continue in the faith, stable and steadfast, not shifting from the hope of the gospel which you heard, which has been preached to every creature under heaven, and of which I, Paul, became a minister.*

Then we have that great theological proclamation of Paul's at Rom 1:16, 17:

> <u>*For I am not ashamed of the gospel: it is the power of God for salvation to everyone who has faith, to the Jew first and*</u>

also to the Greek. *¹⁷ For in it the righteousness of God is revealed through faith for faith; as it is written, "He who through faith is righteous shall live."*

It is not surprising that Paul would come down so stridently on any doctrine or preaching that was more or less than the gospel of Christ!

Major points to learn from this lesson

1. In this section Paul builds on his own experience of opposition in Philippi, and his experience in Rome as a prisoner.
2. Paul was aware that certain false teachers were active in the Philippian church.
3. He encouraged the Philippian Christians to not be discouraged by those who were disrupting the harmony of the church and he encouraged them to not be discouraged by opposition and disrupting tactics.
4. He warned them to proclaim the gospel message without fear in the face of difficulty and opposition just as he had in Philippi and in Rome.
5. Paul drew heavily on his own experiences and example in Philippi and Rome.
6. Paul was concerned that the gospel of Christ, and only the gospel of Christ, would be preached in and under all circumstances.

Discussion points from this lesson

1. When discussing the following points stay within the context of the text at Phil 1:121-18.
2. What may we discern from this lesson were the factors causing the Christians to experience the "blahs" in Philippi?
3. What might be the overriding theme in Paul's exhortation in the text of this lesson?
4. How would you discuss Paul's claim to not be preaching baptism but only the cross of Christ? Does this remove baptism from the gospel? Note Rom 6:1-4.
5. What experiences or attitudes in your own Christian life and witness could be disrupting to deep fellowship in your congregational life?

6. What have you learned from this lesson that might offset such experiences and the "blahs"?
7. From this lesson what have you learned about encouraging your fellow Christians? Stay in the context of the text in this lesson.

Chapter 5: Jesus Christ Our Model for Christian Service

Phil 2:1-11

Paul's Exhortation to the Philippians regarding Humility and Concern for Others: Phil 2:1-4

¹ So if there is any encouragement in Christ, any incentive of love, any participation in the Spirit, any affection and sympathy, 2 complete my joy by being of the same mind, having the same love, being in full accord and of one mind. 3 Do nothing from selfishness or conceit, but in humility count others better than yourselves. 4 Let each of you look not only to his own interests, but also to the interests of others.

Paul gets to the heart of his concern for the Philippian Christians – spiritual "blahs" and a lack of real concern for one another! In every congregation or church there is always the inclination for being overly sensitive or concerned for one's own interests! We might not like the hymns the song leader has chosen, or how the Lord's Supper is conducted.

Phil 2:1. Paul is aware of such a tendency in the Philippian congregation, so he begins by pointing first to Christ, observing that in Christ and from Christ we learn to be sensitive for the needs of others, not simply our own. We should gain confidence and encouragement, an incentive to love, and the ground for harmony which we see in Christ's example.

O'Brien sees the exhortations of this text as forming the heart of the arguments Paul makes in the remainder of the epistle:

> The place and purpose of 2:1–4 within the context of 1:27–2:18 and its relationship to the christological hymn of 2:5–11 also demand attention. It was noted at 1:27 that the apostle focused on one highly significant demand, namely that the readers should conduct their lives in a manner worthy of the gospel of Christ. This would involve them, first of all, standing fast or secure with a common purpose ('in one

spirit') in the face of attacks from outside against the progress of the gospel (1:27–30). Now the apostle looks for a steadfast resistance to all kinds of internal division. 2:1–4 functions as a call to unity, love, and humility within a closely knit section of the letter (1:27–2:18). The Philippians are to be united not only against a common foe but also in heart and mind with one another.[1]

The opening strophe (v. 1) is characterized by a fourfold εἴ τις (τι) together with two substantives in each line. These four brief statements in synonymous parallelism form the basis of the apostle's appeal to the Philippians as he speaks of supernatural, objective realities that have already occurred in their lives. The fourfold εἰ ('if'), which formally introduces four conditional sentences, should be rendered 'since', or 'if, as is indeed the case', and the construction without the verb (most interpreters suggest that ἐστιν should be supplied), together with the sense given, is classical.[2]

Fee observes that the thoughts of Phil 2:1ff indicate that a challenge to the unity within the congregation lay in a genuine Christlike relationship with one another in keeping with the basic message of the gospel:

> This paragraph thus holds the keys to much in this letter, especially regarding Paul's concerns about things on their end, which have undoubtedly been reported to him by Epaphroditus. Although he does not explicitly say so (but cf. 4:2-3), 2:2-3 and 14 imply there are some internal tensions among them; at the same time there are some external pressures being applied, which bid fair to make their situation as God's people in Philippi tenuous. Paul's ultimate concern for them is directly related to his concern for the gospel in Philippi. His obvious hope, as 2:1-2 makes plain, is that his and their long-term friendship and participation together in the gospel will pull them through this twofold crisis.[3]

Silva agrees with Fee:

---

[1] O'Brien, P. T., *The Epistle to the Philippians: a commentary on the Greek text*, Grand Rapids: Eerdmans, 1991, p. 166.
[2] O'Brien, *op. cit.*, p. 165.
[3] Fee, *ibid.*, kindle locations 4949-4954.

Because they have lost, or at least are in danger of losing, the fundamental Christian perspective of joy, the apostle in this letter exhorts them repeatedly to rejoice (2:18; 3:1; 4:4; see introduction, "Distinctive Teaching"). Moreover, Paul reinforces his exhortation by emphasizing the joy that the Philippians have brought to him in spite of his afflictions (1:4). Perhaps Paul recognizes that the key to joy consists in shifting our attention away from ourselves and onto the needs of others. In any case, Paul once again addresses the issue of the Philippians' unity as the one matter that concerns him (see above on monon, 1:27), as the one problem that is preventing him from experiencing full joy with regard to his Philippian brethren.[4]

Paul opens the discussion with the expression *so if there is any encouragement in Christ*. The little conditional expression *so if there is any*, in Greek Εἴ τις, *ei tis*, leads the mind into a series of clauses that suggest several thoughts or topics which form the basis of true Christian fellowship and unity.

Hawthorne and Martin comment on this coordinating conjunction that leads into this interesting list of conditional phrases that follow the initial *if*:

> This verse has four brief clauses, each of which begins with εἰ, "if," and contains two nouns and no verbs. As a result, it presents the translator with unusual difficulties and the commentator with a bewildering number of possibilities of interpretation. For example, to translate these expressions into English as conditional clauses, each beginning with the word "if," does retain something of the rhythm and the rhetorical repetitiveness of the Greek, but it may convey the wrong idea. When Paul introduced each of these clauses with εἰ, "if," he did not intend by this to cast doubt at all on what he was saying. Just the opposite. The construction of these clauses in Greek, introduced by εἰ, is such that it becomes equivalent in meaning to an affirmative statement: *"Since there is …"*[5]

---

[4] Silva, Moisés. *Philippians*, Baker Exegetical Commentary on the New Testament, Baker Publishing Group, kindle edition, 2005, p. 86.
[5] Hawthorne, *ibid.*, p. 82. Cf. also Loh and Nida, *ibid.*, on the problem of a literal translation.

Melick succinctly adds that these four statements form the basis of Paul's mind of Christian community:

> Four statements form the basis of Paul's appeal to the Philippians. The statements are introduced by "if" in both Greek and English. Although the word "if" brings doubt to mind, these clauses express little hesitancy. They should be translated "assuming ... then make my joy complete." All four statements introduce the command of 2:2, and they identify Paul's avenue of approaching the church. *Paul gently reminded the believers of what he and they had in common.*
>
> *The four statements recall the blessings of being in a Christian community.* The first statement is, "If you have any encouragement from being united with Christ." Commentators differ on the precise meaning of the word translated "encouragement" (*paraklēsis*). The Greek word is capable of meaning *encouragement* or *exhortation.* The tone of this section is warm and gentle, *as Paul appealed to their common experience of Christ.* The best understanding of the word seems to be "encouragement" that comes from Christian commitment. Second is the blessing of "comfort from his love." The NIV correctly translates this as affirming Christ's love for his people. The "fellowship with the Spirit" is the third statement of blessing. All agree that this refers to the Holy Spirit. The question is whether this is fellowship brought by the Spirit or fellowship in the Spirit. Finally, there is "tenderness and compassion." Again, these terms refer to the mercies shown them by the Lord. These statements make a strong emotional appeal. Their rhetorical value clearly surfaces, and though Paul approached the Philippians gently here, the combined effect of the statements was powerful. *The church had a common experience of grace, and Paul built upon that in his exhortation.* Since the other three of these qualities seem to be spiritual in nature, it is best to take this as a fellowship the Holy Spirit provides.[6]

Phil 2:3, 4. Christ's example of selfish service and humility and concern for others, upon which Paul will shortly elaborate in profound detail, emphasize the ground of Christian fellowship. The ideal

---

[6] Melick, *ibid.*, p. 93. Emphases mine, IAF.

example of Christian *love* (*agápē*, the desire for the very best for others) arises out of looking not to one's own interests but to the interests of others. Paul exhorts the Philippians to not be selfish and full of their own interests but to be humble in their relationship with their fellow brothers and sisters in Christ.

With the opening thoughts to this pericope Paul got to the heart of the epistle! A remedy for the spiritual "blahs"! The *encouragement of being in Christ, of participation in the Spirit, of affection and sympathy, of joy in being of the same mind, of having the same love, and being in full accord and of one mind*! This text addresses Paul's chief concern for the church at Philippi; their permitting outside influences to impact their Christian witness to the gospel of Christ, their loss of mutual concern for one another, and the loss of the joy of Christian fellowship.

The thoughts of Phil 2:3, 4 resonate with tones of Rom 12:9-18:

> *⁹ Let love be genuine; hate what is evil, hold fast to what is good; 10 love one another with brotherly affection; outdo one another in showing honor. 11 Never flag in zeal, be aglow with the Spirit, serve the Lord. 12 Rejoice in your hope, be patient in tribulation, be constant in prayer. 13 Contribute to the needs of the saints, practice hospitality.*
>
> *14 Bless those who persecute you; bless and do not curse them. 15 Rejoice with those who rejoice, weep with those who weep. 16 Live in harmony with one another; do not be haughty, but associate with the lowly; never be conceited. 17 Repay no one evil for evil, but take thought for what is noble in the sight of all. 18 If possible, so far as it depends upon you, live peaceably with all.*

Christ: The Theological Example of

Humble Christian Service

> *⁵ Have this mind among yourselves, which is yours in Christ Jesus, 6 who, though he was in the form of God, did not count equality with God a thing to be grasped, 7 but emptied himself, taking the form of a servant, being born in the likeness of men. 8 And being found in human form he humbled himself and became obedient unto death, even death on a cross. 9 Therefore God has highly exalted him and bestowed*

> *on him the name which is above every name, 10 that at the name of Jesus every knee should bow, in heaven and on earth and under the earth, 11 and every tongue confess that Jesus Christ is Lord, to the glory of God the Father.*

Phil 2:5-11. This is possibly the most Christocentric pericope in the epistle to the Philippians, and arguably also of the whole New Testament! Most scholars recognize this pericope to be in the form of either an early Christian hymn, or an early confessional statement. This might not be the appropriate place to engage the interesting debate on the origins of this hymn or confession. My point will be to draw attention to the beauty and rhythmic hymnic form of the pericope, and the power of its message.[7]

Peter O'Brien observes regarding this pericope:

> This magnificent passage (vv. 6–11) is an early Christian hymn in honor of Christ. It is the most important section of the letter to the Philippians and provides a marvelous description of Christ's self-humbling in his incarnation and death, together with his subsequent exaltation by God to the place of highest honor.
>
> The paragraph is the most difficult in Philippians to interpret. This is not, however, through lack of secondary literature on vv. 5–11, for there has been a continual flow of studies and articles in the twenty years since R. P. Martin's history of interpretation was first published. Little scholarly consensus has emerged in relation to the origin and authorship of the passage (pre-Pauline, Pauline, or post-Pauline?), its form and structure (hymnic? the number of stanzas?), the conceptual background of the passage (OT, Gnostic myth, general Hellenism, wisdom speculation?), or key exegetical and theological issues. As a result, at several points in the following exposition it has been necessary to treat the more detailed cruxes in appendices, with the major conclusions being summarized in the main text...

---

[7] For detailed discussion on this hymn refer to the commentaries listed in the bibliography. Whether this hymn was written by Paul himself, or was an early traditional hymn is not the point here. We accept it as a major theological piece in which Paul saw much meaning and around which he developed his Christological argument.

> In describing the passage as a 'hymn' it should be noted that the term is not being employed in the modern sense of what we understand by congregational hymns with metrical verses. Nor are we to think in terms of Greek or Semitic poetical metre. The category is used broadly, similar to that of 'creed', and includes dogmatic, confessional, liturgical, polemical, or doxological material.[8]

O'Brien adds however that in spite of its beauty and significance this pericope/hymn has challenged scholars through the centuries!

Phil 2:5-11. Regarding the role of Phil 2:5 in this pericope of hymn O'Brien observes:

> Paul's personal admonition to the Philippians concludes the stirring appeal of vv. 1–4 and at the same time introduces the hymn of vv. 6–11. This verse, a crux interpretum over which there has been and continues to be considerable difference of opinion, 'has essentially a transitional nature', forming a link between the two sections.

In the words of Norman Tom Wright, some texts are densely packed and need careful unloading. This is one of those texts!

Around this pericope a whole theological library has developed through the centuries of Christian theology. In theological jargon this train of thought has been called Kenotic Theology.[9] Primarily Kenotic Theology relates to exploring what divine miraculous powers Jesus must have given up at his incarnation, and when they might have been restored to him. While this is an interesting thought, it is not what this pericope develops and this approach misses the heart of what Paul is discussing in this text. As one of my esteemed professors once said when confronted by a wide variety of opinions and options, *read the text and stay with the text*! The answer to this so-called mystery will become apparent as we work our way through this text and unpack its mysteries. We will learn that it will turn out

---

[8] O'Brien, P. T., *ibid.,* pp. 186–188. Cf also Gerald F. Hawthorne, Ralph P. Martin, *Philippians*; I-Jin Loh, *A Translator's Handbook to Paul's Letter to the Philippians*; Moisés Silva, *Philippians*; Frank S. Thielman, *Philippians*; Richard R. Melick, Jr.; *Philippians, Colossians, Philemon;* Gordon D. Fee, *Paul's Letter to the Philippians.*
[9] Cf. John H. Gerstner, "Kenosis," *Baker's Dictionary of Theology*, Grand Rapids: Baker Book House, 1960/83, pp. 308f; Alan Richardson, *A Dictionary of Christian Theology*, London: SCM Press, 1969, pp. 59ff, for an excellent discussion of Kenotic Theology in a lengthy article of Christology in the debate regarding the divine-human nature of Jesus in the context of his incarnation.

not to be as mysterious a topic as proposed by some Kenotic Theology theories! Bear with me!

Phil 2:5: Returning to the text under discussion we pick up the heart of Paul's argument. In the previous pericope, Phil 1:12-30, he had used his own example as an encouragement to the Philippians to take heart; now at Phil 2:5 he arrives at the main theological point he is making in this exhortation, adopting the mind and attitude of Christ: "*Have this mind among yourselves, which is yours in Christ Jesus ...*" In the words that follow in clear concise thoughts Paul defines what he means by the mind of Christ which he is encouraging the Philippians to replicate in their own lives.

To drive home the extent of his exhortation, Paul begins by stressing the force of his argument, Jesus' great example of humble service and concern for others.

Phil 2:6. *First*, though Jesus was fully equal to God in his divinity[10] he was willing to surrender this, to empty himself of that divine royal privilege, and in his human form become a servant!

Elsewhere, Paul had written of Jesus:

> *He is the image of the invisible God, the first-born of all creation;* [16] *for in him all things were created, in heaven and on earth, visible and invisible, whether thrones or dominions or principalities or authorities—all things were created through him and for him.* [17] *He is before all things, and in him all things hold together.* [18] *He is the head of the body, the church; he is the beginning, the first-born from the dead, that in everything he might be pre-eminent.* [19] *For in him all the fulness of God was pleased to dwell,* [20] *and through him to reconcile to himself all things, whether on earth or in heaven, making peace by the blood of his cross ...* [9] *For in him the whole fulness of deity dwells bodily,* [10] *and you have come to fulness of life in him, who is the head of all rule and authority.*[11]

"*Though he was in the form of God he counted not equality with God a thing to be grasped.*" That the human Jesus was equal in every sense to God, and had been so eternally, is perhaps one of the most

---

[10] Cf. John 1:1-3; Col 1:15-19; 2:9.
[11] Col 1:15-19; 2:9–10.

striking and difficult thoughts to get one's arms around! Fully human and fully divine![12]

We have become so familiar with the fact that Jesus walked around in human form that we tend to bypass the enormity of Jesus' divine incarnation. Karl Barth, noted Swiss/German theologian of the 1st half of the 20th century claimed that the incarnation was the greatest of all of God's acts of enormous love and grace. In fact, Barth made the incarnation of Jesus the beginning point and foundation of his extensive theology.[13]

The Apostle John expressed the heart of incarnational theology well when he wrote:

> *For God so loved the world that he gave his only Son, that whoever believes in him should not perish but have eternal life. ^{17} For God sent the Son into the world, not to condemn the world, but that the world might be saved through him.* (John 3:16).

That Jesus was willing to give up equality with God, living in a special eternal relationship with God, and a position of sovereignty and power in which with God he had with sovereign power created everything that exists, is in itself amazing (cf. John 1:1, 2; Heb 1:1-3; 1 Cor 8:6).

Among the many striking biblical statements regarding Jesus' incarnation I find Heb 1:1-3 to be most expressive of this amazing act of God's love and grace. The preacher writes:

> *In many and various ways God spoke of old to our fathers by the prophets; ^{2} but in these last days he has spoken to us by a Son, whom he appointed the heir of all things, through whom also he created the world. ^{3} He reflects the glory of God*

---

[12] Cf. Wolfhart Pannenberg, *Jesus-God and Man*, London: SCM Press, 1968, for an excellent discussion on the full divinity of Jesus; also Donald Guthrie, "Christology," *New Testament Theology*, Leicester England: Inter-Varsity Press, 1981, pp. 219ff; Joel B. Green, Scot McKnight, I, Howard Marshall, "Christology", *Dictionary of Jesus and the Gospels*, Leicester, England: Inter-Varsity Press, 1992, *passim*; O'Brian, *ibid.*, pp. 205ff; Melick, *ibid*, pp 101ff; Carson, *ibid.*, kindle locations, 509ff; Fee, *ibid.*, kindle locations, 5842ff; Silva, *ibid.*, pp. 91ff; and Thielman, *ibid*, pp. 109ff.

[13] Karl Barth's bibliography is so extensive that in the context of this study we will reference only his magisterial *Church Dogmatics*, vols 1-4, passim, and Ian A. Fair, *The Theology of Wolfhart Pannenberg as a Reaction to Dialectical; Theology*, *passim*.

and bears the very stamp of his nature, upholding the universe by his word of power.

In spite of his eternal glory and divinity, in his incarnation we find the divine Son, Jesus, revealed as a baby in his mother's arms, the son of a carpenter in Nazareth. In fact, as one scholar expressed it, the divine Son, Jesus, became a marginalized Jew in a world dominated by the religious hierarchy of Judaism, and the political power of Rome.[14] Since eternity he had been fully equal to the almighty God and now without restraint he was willing to become equal in every sense with humanity as a simple human, the son of a village carpenter, being subject to all of the physical weaknesses of humanity. Surely, we can call this a living sign of Amazing Grace!

A dominant philosophical quasi-religious mood of the 1st and early 2nd century CE, which some have termed Gnosticism, seriously questioned Jesus' incarnation as the divine living in human form. Their argument was that the human Jesus remained human in every sense of humanity, and that the divine Christ had only used Jesus' physical body for a period of time.[15] The Apostle John boldly called the consequent denial of the miraculous virgin birth of Jesus and his full deity *the antichrist.* Cf. 1 John 2:18-25 and 1 John 4:1-3:

> 1 John 2:18. *Children, it is the last hour; and as you have heard that antichrist is coming, so now many antichrists have come; therefore we know that it is the last hour. ^{19} They went out from us, but they were not of us; for if they had been of us, they would have continued with us; but they went out, that it might be plain that they all are not of us. ^{20} But you have been anointed by the Holy One, and you all know. ^{21} I write to you, not because you do not know the truth, but because you know it, and know that no lie is of the truth. ^{22} <u>Who is the liar but he who denies that Jesus is the Christ? This is the antichrist, he who denies the Father and the Son.</u> ^{23} No one who denies the Son has the Father. He who confesses the Son has the Father also. ^{24} Let what you heard from the beginning abide in you. If*

---

[14] John P. Meier, *A Marginalized Jew: Rethinking the Historical Jesus*, New York: Doubleday, 1991.

[15] I recognize this is a simplification of the gnostic challenge to the full divinity of Jesus in human form, but I mention it only to demonstrate the point that even within the early era of the Christian world, understanding the full divinity of Jesus, the son of Joseph, posed serious challenges.

what you heard from the beginning abides in you, then you will abide in the Son and in the Father. ^{25} And this is what he has promised us, eternal life ...I John 4:1. *Beloved, do not believe every spirit, but test the spirits to see whether they are of God; for many false prophets have gone out into the world. ^{2} By this you know the Spirit of God: <u>every spirit which confesses that Jesus Christ has come in the flesh is of God, ^{3} and every spirit which does not confess Jesus is not of God. This is the spirit of antichrist</u>, of which you heard that it was coming, and now it is in the world already.*

Paul stressed that Jesus' willingness to leave the supreme existence of equality with God to become fully human was not something he did reluctantly. He did not cling to his divine nature and position with God, or as Paul aptly expresses it, *though he was in the form of God, did not count equality with God a thing to be grasped* ... The word *grasped* derives from the Greek ἁρπαγμός, *harpagmós* which denotes *to seize with force* or *hold onto with force*.[16] Jesus willingly gave up his exalted position with God, which he had clearly enjoyed since before creation, and willingly and humbly became human.

In a magnificent theological summary of this, John explained the mystery of Jesus' full divinity and divine incarnation:

^{1} <u>In the beginning was the Word, and the Word was with God, and the Word was God</u>. ^{2} He was in the beginning with God; ^{3} all things were made through him, and without him was not anything made that was made. ^{4} In him was life, and the life was the light of men. ^{5} The light shines in the darkness, and the darkness has not overcome it ...

^{9} The true light that enlightens every man was coming into the world. ^{10} He was in the world, and the world was made through him, yet the world knew him not. ^{11} He came to his own home, and his own people received him not. ^{12} But to all who received him, who believed in his name, he gave power to become children of God; ^{13} who were born, not of blood nor of the will of the flesh nor of the will of man, but of God.

^{14} <u>And the Word became flesh and dwelt among us, full of grace and truth; we have beheld his glory, glory as of the only</u>

---

[16] Zodhiates, *ibid.* Cf. also Gerhard Kittel, *Theological Dictionary of the New Testament.*

> *Son from the Father.* <u>*¹⁵*</u> *(John bore witness to him, and cried, "This was he of whom I said, 'He who comes after me ranks before me, for he was before me.'") ¹⁶ And from his fulness*[17] *have we all received, grace upon grace. ¹⁷ For the law was given through Moses; grace and truth came through Jesus Christ. ¹⁸ No one has ever seen God; the only Son, who is in the bosom of the Father, he has made him known.* [18]

Phil 2:7. Paul's next statement at Phil 2:7 has generated an extensive library of theological thought designated as Kenotic[19] Theology. The scope of kenotic theology ranges over a wide range of religious thought, having impacted Roman Catholic, Eastern Orthodox, Gnostic, and Protestant theology. In short, kenotic theology addresses the miraculous nature of the incarnation, and seeks to understand how the divine Christ could indwell the human form of Jesus without surrendering some of his divine power. This implied that somehow in his incarnation Jesus gave up certain of his divine powers or rights. Questions such as "Did the boy Jesus know he was God?" "Did the boy Jesus demonstrate his divine miraculous powers?" "What divine and miraculous powers did Jesus give up in becoming human?" Illustrating the early nature of this question, a 2nd or 3rd century Gnostic Gospel, *The Gospel of Thomas*, found at Nag Hammadi in Northern Egypt in 1945, included the story of the boy Jesus entertaining his friends by making clay pigeons and throwing them into the air, upon which they flew away! The story is obviously fictitious, but it demonstrates the nature of the problem the incarnation created for some.

Since the proposed "kenotic theology" is set in a text of such profound importance, and since it has been of interest to this epistle for centuries, I am including several observations from recent scholarship.

The text we have in mind, Phil 2:6, speaks of the almost unfathomable example we have in *Christ Jesus emptying himself*:

---

[17] The Greek word *fulness*, πλήρωμα, *plḗrōma*, in the gnostic and other theological traditions carried within it *claims to divinity*. Cf Zodhiates, *op. cit.*, πλήρωμα, *plḗrōma*; to make full, fill, fill up ... Generally, as in John 1:16; Eph. 3:19; Col. 2:9, the fullness refers to the plenitude of divine perfections. Cf Kittel, *ibid*, pp. 303f.
[18] John 1:1–18.
[19] Zodhiates, *op. cit.*, The word *kenotic* derives from the Greek κενόω *kenóō* to empty, void, to make empty, falsify, be fallacious.

> *"who, though he was in the form of God, did not count equality with God a thing to be grasped, ⁷ but emptied himself, taking the form of a servant, being born in the likeness of men."*

The expression *emptied himself* is derived from the Greek ἑαυτὸν ἐκένωσεν, *heauton ekenōsev*, the word of concern being ἐκένωσεν, *ekenōsev*, an aorist indicative of κενόω, *kenóō*. Regarding κενόω, *kenóō*, Zodhiates observes:

> The use in Phil. 2:7 is of great theological importance. It refers to Jesus Christ as emptying Himself at the time of His incarnation, denoting the beginning of His self–humiliation in verse eight. In order to understand what is meant by Jesus' emptying Himself, the whole passage (Phil. 2:6–8) must be examined.[20]

O'Brien observes regarding this mysterious expression:

> ... ἀλλὰ ἑαυτὸν ἐκένωσεν. In sharp contrast (note the strong adversative ἀλλά, 'on the contrary') to the way that might have been chosen, Christ 'emptied himself'. This is a most striking phrase which has no convincing parallel in the whole of Greek literature. The emphatic position of ἑαυτόν ('himself') and the form of the verb (an aorist active) strongly suggest that this act of 'emptying' was voluntary on the part of the preexistent Christ.
>
> κενόω in secular Greek meant 'to empty, make empty' in a literal sense, and then metaphorically 'to make of no effect'. In the LXX the simple form of the verb is found only twice (Je. 14:2; 15:9), in a metaphorical sense meaning 'to languish'. κενόω is used only five times in the NT. Three of these are in the passive voice and the sense required is clearly metaphorical: at Rom. 4:14 it has to do with faith being made void, in 1 Cor. 1:17 regarding the cross of Christ and at 2 Cor. 9:3 of Paul's boasting as an apostle. The remaining two instances of κενόω (1 Cor. 9:15; Phil. 2:7) are in the active voice, and a metaphorical sense holds good for 1 Cor. 9:15, where κενώσει means 'deprive'. Thus, in four of the five NT occurrences of the verb it bears a metaphorical sense; the

---

[20] Zodhiates, *ibid*.

balance of probability lies in favor of a figurative connotation at Phil. 2:7 as well.

Accordingly, it has been suggested that this enigmatic expression is a 'poetic, hymn-like way of saying that Christ poured out himself, putting himself totally at the disposal of people'. This meaning, it is argued, suits the entire passage (2:3–11) with its exhortation to humility. Again, ἑαυτὸν ἐκένωσεν has been interpreted metaphorically to refer to Christ making himself powerless in the sense of accepting that vocation which led to the real humiliation of his incarnation and finally his death on the cross. Either suggestion makes good sense, though our preference is the latter (see below).

The meaning of ἑαυτὸν ἐκένωσεν is defined more precisely in the two participial phrases that follow, namely μορφὴν δούλου λαβών ('taking the form of a slave') and ἐν ὁμοιώματι ἀνθρώπων γενόμενος (being found in human form') ... since the two aorist participles λαβών and γενόμενος are coincident with the finite verb ἐκένωσεν and both are modal, describing the manner in which Christ 'emptied himself.'[21]

On kenotic theology, Hawthorne and Martin include an extensive Excursus which I have included for reference.

It is the insistence on the reality of Christ's humanness and the use of the verb κενοῦν, "to empty," in Phil 2:7 that gave rise to and provided the name for the kenotic theory of the incarnation. This ancient theory (going back to H. Grotius in the seventeenth century), as recently expounded by Collange ... claims that "at the incarnation Christ divested himself of the 'relative' attributes of deity, omniscience, omnipresence and omnipotence, but retained the 'essential attributes' of holiness, love and righteousness." Such a theory, in spite of its worthy motive of attempting to do justice to the reality of Christ's humanity and his being-in-God, cannot be supported by the statements in Phil 2 for the following reasons: (1) The significant statements regarding Christ's kenosis are found in a hymn using mythopoetic idioms (2:6–11). (2) The hymn form cautions against building a doctrine

---

[21] O'Brien, *ibid.*, pp. 216–217.

on any single statement to be found in it. For, like a poem, the hymn is composed not to be analyzed word by word, but to be understood in its entirety. The full impact of its meaning, therefore, is found not in the part but the whole, and the whole thrust of the hymn is alien to the issues raised by the kenoticists ... (3) Although the verb κενοῦν, "to empty," is used here (v 7), its meaning is too imprecise to permit one to say that Christ emptied himself of certain divine attributes. In fact, as was pointed out above, the Philippian text does not say that Christ gave up anything. Rather it says that he added to himself that which he did not have before— "the form of a slave," "the likeness of human beings." Thus the implication is that at the incarnation Christ became more than God, if this is conceivable, not less than God. Yet that "more than" quality, represented by the preposition ὑπέρ (as in 2:9: "*more than* highly exalted him"), awaits the enthronement and gives point to the conclusion that the humbled Christ showed obedience, in a slavelike manner, by his destined death. It was only later (διὸ καί, "as a consequence, therefore") that he was elevated to lordship over the cosmos, which is not in view in v 6 since it traces back Christ's eternal, pretemporal state to a time when there was no cosmos to rule. And it is this exaltation that gives uniqueness to the Christ-event, making the imitation view difficult. What Tasker ... says of the death of Christ— "There is only one Calvary"—is just as applicable to the entire range of Christ's existence.

It is impossible to explain such a mystery—that the one who was on par with God could also be a human person to the fullest, a truly genuine human being possessing all the potential for physical, mental, social, and spiritual growth that is proper to humanity (Luke 2:52), and be both at the same time—divine and human, God and a human being. Here, of course, speaks the voice of creedal Christianity with Chalcedonian overtones. Nevertheless, the Philippian hymn seems clearly to set forth just such a paradox and affirm it but does not try to explain it. Hence, anyone coming to the text in the hope of interpreting it must exercise the same kind of balance and reserve, neither tampering with anything relating to the divinity of Christ, nor calling into question any aspect of the reality of his humanity ... see also G. F. Hawthorne, *The Presence and the Power: The Significance of the Holy Spirit in the Life and Ministry of Jesus* ... 1991; reprint ... 2003]).[22]

After making the challenging, albeit enigmatic statement that Jesus counted not equality with God a thing to be fiercely defended and that he had emptied himself of all claims to superiority, Paul defines the nature of this emptying as Jesus *taking on the form of a servant, being born in the likeness of men*, Phil 2:7b.

As we focus on the hymnic and emotive nature of the pericope itself it becomes obvious that Paul's use of this hymn serves as the foundation of what he was encouraging the Philippians to emulate in their relationship with one another, emptying themselves of pride and position and becoming servants of one another.

Phil 2:7. The extent of Jesus' emptying himself was not only in his becoming human but in the extent in which he became human, he took on *the form of a servant*! This in itself distanced him from the Jewish leaders who expected the Messiah to come in the form of a king! He came in the form of the lowest form of servant, as a δοῦλος, *doúlos, a bonded slave!* Zodhiates defines this as:

> "a slave, one who is in a permanent relation of servitude to another, his will being altogether consumed in the will of the other ... Generally one serving, bound to serve, in bondage.[23]

Hawthorne and Martin observe regarding the meaning of δοῦλος, *doúlos* in this great text:

> "If the incident from the life of Jesus where Jesus puts himself in the place of the slave and washes his disciples' feet (John 13) played any part in shaping this hymn, if the context in which the hymn is inserted presents a call to serve one another, then δοῦλος, "slave," emphasizes that in the incarnation Christ entered the stream of human life as a slave, that is, as a person without advantage, with no rights or privileges of his own, for the express purpose of placing himself completely at the service of all humankind ...[24]

---

[22] Hawthorne, and Martin, *ibid*, p. 121.
[23] Zodhiates, *ibid*.
[24] Hawthorne, *ibid*, p. 119.

O'Brien sums up the extensive discussion[25] that has evolved around the primary meaning of δοῦλος, *doúlos* as follows:

> We conclude with a summary evaluation. Bearing in mind that the apostle is writing to Christian readers in Philippi with a pagan past, it seems best, on balance, to understand the expression μορφὴν δούλου λαβών against the background of slavery in contemporary society. Slavery pointed to the extreme deprivation of one's rights, even those relating to one's own life and person. When Jesus emptied himself by embracing the divine vocation and becoming incarnate he become a slave, without any rights whatever. He did not exchange the nature or form of God for that of a slave; instead, he displayed the nature or form of God in the nature or form of a slave, thereby showing clearly not only what his character was like, but also what it meant to be God. A particularly telling example of this, as Hawthorne and Bruce note, was Jesus' washing the disciples' feet and drying them with a towel he had tied around his waist (Jn. 13:3–5). Jesus' extreme act of humble service became the pattern of true servanthood, and it is understandable how Christian vocabulary would then come to reflect this, as Hurtado points out. But the action of Jesus serves as the model and explains the servant language.[26]

Phil 2:8. Bringing his example of Jesus' incarnation home to the level of the Philippians Paul adds, "*And being found in human form he humbled himself and became obedient unto death, even death on a cross.*" No longer in divine glory but now in self-effacing human form Jesus humbled himself, being an obedient slave even to the point of being willing to die a human criminal's death for his "master" God. Crucifixion was the penalty for the worst form of criminals in the Roman system and Jesus was willing to humble himself beyond normal reason. The extent of Jesus' humility in death would not have been lost on the Philippians who would have been very aware of the penalty and cruel nature of crucifixion. Paul's point in mentioning Jesus' death on the cross was not to make a soteriological theme here but to stress the extent of the humility and sense of service

---

[25] All of the scholarly works on Philippians have discussed in detail the wide-ranging views relating to this servanthood. The conclusions of Hawthorne, Martin, Bruce, and Moule seem to be the most applicable to the context of this hymn.
[26] O'Brien, *ibid.*, pp. 223–224.

demonstrated by Jesus which Paul was exhorting the Philippians to emulate in favor of their brothers and sisters in Christ.

Phil 2:9. The result of Jesus' self-emptying obedient humility was that God had *highly exalted him and bestowed on him the name which is above every name.* The expression of Jesus being bestowed with a name that is far above every name has roots in the ancient cultural and theological meaning of *name/character*. Zodhiates observes that the expression implies more than identity and stressed character, an honorable appellation, or a title.[27]

Zodhiates' comments are helpful, but as O'Brien observes the full meaning of this new name includes conferring on Jesus the name and character of Lord, κύριος *kúrios*, which was the Greek equivalent of YHWH, God's own name![28]

Unfortunately, the English reader will unknowingly miss the Hebrew/Greek distinctions in the name YHWH and κύριος *kúrios*!

Melick observes regarding the nuances of the honor given to Jesus as Lord, κύριος *kúrios*!

> Ultimately, every creature in the universe will acknowledge who Jesus is. Two concerns must be discussed: the meaning of "at the name of Jesus" and the description of which persons acknowledge him. The phrase "at the name of Jesus" may mean that he is the object of worship, that he is the medium of worship, or that he provides the occasion and focus of worship. The context clearly reveals that Jesus is to be the object of worship, as the name "Lord" and his exalted position indicate. That rules out Jesus as a medium of worship, but more may be required by this expression. In fact, more is intended. Wherever Jesus' name (and character) has authority, he will be worshiped.
>
> Christ acted selflessly to accomplish the will of God. He even died to provide salvation as a part of the divine plan. God chose to honor him, determining that Christ would be the focus of the Godhead in its interactions with creation. Because of Jesus' actions, the way to honor God is to honor Christ.

---

[27] Zodhiates, *ibid*.
[28] Zodhiates, *op. cit.*, κύριος *kúrios* … might, power. It can be translated as Lord, master, owner. In the NT it is the Greek equivalent for the OT Hebrew, Jehovah.

Even so, the glory Christ receives is a glory given to the Father. [29]

O'Brien discusses at length the implication of this *new name* bestowed on Jesus who had emptied himself by becoming a slave to humankind:

> But the expression τὸ ὄνομα τὸ ὑπὲρ πᾶν ὄνομα, in our judgment, is best interpreted along other lines. In ancient thought a 'name' was employed not only as a means of distinguishing one person from another but also as 'a means of revealing the inner being, the true nature of that individual' (cf. Gn. 25:26; 1 Sa. 25:25). As Bauer put it, a name represents 'something real, a piece of the very nature of the personality whom it designates, that partakes in his qualities and his powers'. Here in v. 9 ὄνομα is not used simply of an individual designation as a proper name. The phrase ὑπὲρ πᾶν ὄνομα ('above every [other] name') shows that something additional is in view. Older commentators who sought to interpret τὸ ὄνομα ('the name') simply of a personal designation given to the glorified Christ missed this important point regarding all the qualities and powers that give meaning and substance to the title.
>
> The name (τὸ ὄνομα is definite) [is] greater than any other that God conferred on Jesus as a gracious gift (ἐκαρίσατο) is his own name, κύριος ('Lord'), in its most sublime sense, that designation used in the LXX to represent the personal name of the God of Israel, that is, *Yahweh*. The reasons for interpreting τὸ ὄνομα as κύριος are: (1) in the ἵνα clause of vv. 10–11, which is subordinate to the main clause in v. 9, Jesus is identified with κύριος (Yahweh), the one to whom universal homage is given (Is. 45:23); (2) it is best to regard τῷ ὀνόματι Ἰησοῦ and τὸ ὄνομα τὸ ὑπὲρ πᾶν ὄνομα as juxtaposed; (3) for a Jew like Paul the superlative name was 'Yahweh'. Since the phrase in v. 10 can mean 'the name of Jesus' it is best to understand it as referring to the name 'Yahweh'; and (4) κύριος gives a symmetry to the hymn: θεός (2:6) becomes δοῦλος (v. 7) and is exalted to be κύριος (v. 11).

---

[29] Melick, *ibid.*, pp. 107–109.

This bestowal by God is the rarest of all honours, in view of his assertion in Is. 42:8: 'I am the Lord (κύριος), that is my name', that is, mine and no one else's. Further, in the light of the above remarks God not only gave Jesus 'a designation which distinguished him from all other beings, a title which outranked all other titles'. He also conferred on him all that 'coincided with that title giving substance and meaning to it'.[33] In his exalted state Jesus has a new rank involving the exercise of universal lordship. This gain was in official, not essential, glory since Jesus did not become divine through exaltation. All authority in heaven and on earth were his by nature as well as by gift (Mt. 28:18; cf. Eph. 1:20–21).[30]

The dramatic contrast between *doúlos* and *kúrios*, absolute humility and transcendent glory would be one the Philippians would clearly understand.

Phil 2:10, 11. A secondary consequence of Jesus' exaltation would be that *at the name of Jesus every knee should bow, in heaven and on earth and under the earth, [11] and every tongue confess that Jesus Christ is Lord, to the glory of God the Father*.

In the eschatological end of all creation all will acknowledge the supreme authority and glory of Jesus' role in the godhead. Every nation and tongue will confess that he is YHWH, everything that God is!

Paul's point was that Philippian pride and failure to honor one another in service and love would only bring disgrace to the church in Philippi, and to the true nature of Jesus and his disciples, and to the glory of God.

We recognize that we within our limited human horizons cannot yet see the glorious eschatological future since we are limited by our humanness and understanding of the trinitarian nature of God. But Paul has revealed to us by revelation that all who confess Jesus' full divinity and emulate his humble service will one day see the mystery of the godhead, revealed to us in this life in three "persons," unfolded as one God, YHWH, in all of his mysterious glory.

---

[30] O'Brien, *ibid.*, pp. 237–238.

Major points to learn from this lesson

1. This is perhaps one of the most significant texts in Scripture discussing Christian discipleship - being Christlike as a humble servant to others.
2. Joy in Christianity comes through humble Christian service to others.
3. The message is both personal and congregational in its message regarding unity and fellowship.
4. Christ and God are our models for Christian service – God in Christ in love humbled himself to become human and our servant.
5. God as Christ living in us should result in humble service to others.
6. Christians are to share in Christ's example of emptying themselves in loving service to others.
7. Kenotic theology must be interpreted as an example of emptying self in humble service to others.
8. The result of humbly giving self in service to others is bringing honor to God and Jesus as YHWH.

Discussion points from this lesson

1. What do you see from this text as being the key to joy in Christianity?
2. What did Paul mean when he said that Christ emptied himself?
3. What did Paul mean when he claimed that God had made Christ Lord? What did the Greek word *kúrios* for *Lord* mean to the Hebrew mind?
4. Can you give three Scriptural texts that claim that Jesus Christ was fully equal to God? Refer to the comments above on Phil 2:9!

Chapter 6: Paul's Encouragement to the Philippians to Mature in their Christian Witness

Phil 2:12-30

> *Therefore, my beloved, as you have always obeyed, so now, not only as in my presence but much more in my absence, work out your own salvation with fear and trembling;* [13] *for God is at work in you, both to will and to work for his good pleasure.*
>
> [14] *Do all things without grumbling or questioning,* [15] *that you may be blameless and innocent, children of God without blemish in the midst of a crooked and perverse generation, among whom you shine as lights in the world,* [16] *holding fast the word of life, so that in the day of Christ I may be proud that I did not run in vain or labor in vain.* [17] *Even if I am to be poured as a libation upon the sacrificial offering of your faith, I am glad and rejoice with you all.* [18] *Likewise you also should be glad and rejoice with me.*

Paul's attachment to the Philippian church surfaces in the opening words of this exhortation, *Therefore, my beloved* .... The rhetorical key *therefore* ties what Paul is going to ask of the Philippians back to central thought of the previous pericope, Jesus' remarkable example of humble service. The theme of Paul's relationship with the Philippians resonates throughout the epistle and is perfectly expressed in the words *my beloved brethren*! He is well aware of their previous obedience to the gospel call and reminds them of this, *as you have always obeyed in my presence,* do so *now!* Obedience in the presence of one's mentor is easier than in the absence of the mentor, but Paul encourages them to act just as though he were present with them.

Although this may not be the best place to develop this thought, Paul was aware of the fact of, or implication of the apostolic "presence" in his epistles. This point was one that the early church respected just as we are aware of the presence of God through his Holy Spirit the Word of God.

Paul's next statement and exhortation is intriguing! He urged them to *work out your own salvation with fear and trembling*! The expression *work out your own salvation* does not imply that they should cognitively and personally determine for themselves what their salvation should be, nor was he encouraging a works ethic for salvation. The expression is a present middle/passive imperative that derives from the Greek κατεργάζομαι, *katergázomai*, which means *to bring about, to accomplish, to bring to its end, to carry out a task until it is finished, to energize, to accomplish completely.*[1]

Hawthorne and Martin observe:

> The verb Paul uses, κατεργάζεσθαι, has the sense of working at something until it is brought to completion, hence "to accomplish," "to achieve," "to bring about" ... Its tense is present, which heightens this idea, denoting not so much present time as continuous action. Paul in effect commands the Philippians to keep working and never to let up until their salvation (σωτηρία) is achieved.[2]

O'Brien notes:

> τὴν ἑαυτῶν σωτηρίαν κατεργάζεσθε. 'Work out your own salvation'. Each of the individual words in this expression is well known in the NT; yet their combination here is unique.[3]

Although there are some commentators who see this admonition as a corporate one to the congregation as a whole fulfilling its obligations, this is not the case! O'Brien is correct in pointing to the personal obligation of the Christians in Philippi to work out their salvation which he knows was in fact permitting the working of God in their lives. Paul reminded the Philippians of this in the next verse. They were to do this *with fear and trembling*! O'Brien adds:

> ἑαυτῶν σωτηρίαν κατεργάζεσθε is a demand to make that salvation fruitful in the here and now as the graces of Christ or the fruit of the Spirit (Gal. 5:22–23) are produced in their lives. It involves continually living in a manner worthy of the gospel of Christ (Phil. 1:27) or 'the continual translating into action of the principles of the gospel that they had believed'. Paul has in mind a 'continuous, sustained, strenuous effort', which is elsewhere described under the imagery of a pursuit, a following after, a pressing on, a contest, a fight, or a race (Phil. 3:12; cf. Rom. 14:19; 1 Cor. 9:24–27; 1 Tim. 6:12).

---

[1] Zodhiates, *ibid.*
[2] Hawthorne and Martin, *Philippians*, p. 140.
[3] O'Brien, *The Epistle to the Philippians: a Commentary on the Greek Text*, p. 276.

Further, to speak of believers being responsible for the outworking of their personal salvation in their day-to-day living in no way denies that this σωτηρία is an act of God (contra argument ... above). In precisely the same way 'make your calling and election sure' (2 Pet. 1:10) does not suggest that election is not God's act.[4]

Paul thus encourages the Philippians *to energize* and *bring to maturity or completion the salvation which God had begun in their lives* and which they now must continue to develop toward maturity in Christ through Christian love for one another and service. O'Brien again summarizes this well:

> Such an outworking of the gospel in their day-to-day living has in view the approaching day of Christ when their salvation will be complete (cf. Rom. 13:11). Furthermore, this appropriate behavior clearly involves them in responsibilities to one another (e.g., pursuing unity through humility), as the preceding and subsequent admonitions show (2:1–4, 14, etc.). But their responsibilities to one another or to the outside world (e.g., 2:15–16) are not to be confused with the content of the eschatological salvation itself.[5]

Paul's next exhortation adds a note of seriousness and importance; *work out your own salvation <u>with fear and trembling for God is at work in you</u>, both to will and to work for his good pleasure. First*, the coupling of *fear and trembling* in Greek, φόβου καὶ τρόμου, *phobou kai tromou* is a form of hendiadys in which the second noun, *trembling*, becomes an adjectival expression which defines or enlarges on the first noun, *fear*.

The juxtaposition of these two nouns in a formulaic sense has engendered considerable discussion among some scholars with some adopting a non-theistic humanistic approach, but O'Brien is correct in rejecting this view:

> μετὰ φόβου καὶ τρόμου is the second phrase modifying the principal verb κατεργάζεσθε and indicates the manner in which the readers are to complete their salvation, namely 'with fear and trembling'. But with what kind of 'fear'? The φόβος word-group in Greek carries as wide a range of

---

[4] O'Brien, *op. cit.*, p. 279. Eschatological salvation refers to the salvation that will be ours when Jesus returns at the end of the age.
[5] O'Brien, *op. cit.*, pp. 279, 280.

meanings as the English 'fear' and could denote 'alarm', 'fright', or 'dismay' in the face of danger, as well as 'reverence' or 'respect' in the presence of fellow humans or God. τρόμος meant 'trembling' or 'quivering' from fear, and was often coupled with φόβος to 'picture a person standing with quivering fear or trembling awe before someone or something'. The two nouns φόβος and τρόμος appear together in the LXX on a number of occasions, almost as a stereotyped expression, and usually refer to the fear of human beings in the presence of God and his mighty acts ...At Is. 19:16 'fear and trembling' describes the future reaction of the Egyptians to the hand of the Lord raised against them in judgment, while in Ps. 2:11 the appropriate response of the rebellious nations and rulers of the earth to the Lord's decisive action of installing his Son and of warning them of imminent destruction is to serve him 'with fear' and to 'rejoice with trembling' ... However, even there, the dread is prompted by God's decree and results from his mighty interventions.

Within the NT Paul is the only writer to use the expression 'fear and trembling', namely at 1 Cor. 2:3; 2 Cor. 7:15; Eph. 6:5, and Phil. 2:12 ... However, an examination of the other contexts in the Pauline corpus where φόβος καὶ τρόμος appears suggests that the phrase has to do with an attitude of due reverence and awe in the presence of God, a godly fear of the believer in view of the final day. It is not the slavish terror of the unbeliever; nor is it an attitude oriented solely towards humans...[6]

The thought of working in a close relationship with God should be driven by ultimate respect, fear, and awe reminds one of two other Pauline texts. Both of these texts speak of respect for the working of the Holy Spirit of God in the life of Christians. 1 Thess 5:16-22 and Eph 4:29-32:

> 1 Thess 5:16-22: *"Rejoice always, [17] pray constantly, [18] give thanks in all circumstances; for this is the will of God in Christ Jesus for you. [19] <u>Do not quench the Spirit</u>, [20] do not despise prophesying, [21] but test everything; hold fast what is good, [22] abstain from every form of evil."*

---

[6] O'Brien, *op. cit.*, p. 282.

> Eph 4:29-32: *"Let no evil talk come out of your mouths, but only such as is good for edifying, as fits the occasion, that it may impart grace to those who hear. ³⁰ And <u>do not grieve the Holy Spirit of God</u>, in whom you were sealed for the day of redemption. ³¹ Let all bitterness and wrath and anger and clamor and slander be put away from you, with all malice, ³² and be kind to one another, tenderhearted, forgiving one another, as God in Christ forgave you."*

The sobering thought of this Philippian text reminds us of, and rekindles respect for the powerful working of God on our lives such as in our new birth into the kingdom which Jesus spoke of to Nicodemus as a *new birth from above*[7] involving the working of the Holy Spirit (John 3:1-6). God is not only at work in our lives, but also wills to work in us for his good pleasure.

In summary, the Philippians needed seriously to actively energize, move forward and mature the saving work God had begun in their lives. But they also needed to respect his wish to be continually active in their lives *for his good pleasure*. To nonchalantly react to God's willingness to work in their lives was the equivalent of carelessly denying the working of the Holy Spirit which carries serious consequences! We are reminded of Jesus' rebuke of the Pharisees at Matt 12:28-32 that to deny the working of the Holy Spirit is an unforgivable sin! Christians should approach the working of God in their lives therefore *with fear and trembling and with ultimate respect*.

Paul's exhortation to the Philippians was specifically related to the news which Epaphroditus had brought to him; the members were not getting along very well. There was some internal bickering among them!

> *¹⁴ Do all things without grumbling or questioning, ¹⁵ that you may be blameless and innocent, children of God without blemish in the midst of a crooked and perverse generation, among whom you shine as lights in the world, ¹⁶ holding fast the word of life, so that in the day of Christ I may be proud that I did not run in vain or labor in vain. ¹⁷Even if I am to be poured as a libation upon the sacrificial offering of your faith,*

---

[7] The Greek word ἄνωθεν, *ánōthen* can mean both *anew* or *from above*! Cf Zodhiates, *ibid*.

> *I am glad and rejoice with you all. ¹⁸ Likewise you also should be glad and rejoice with me.*

That Paul was concerned with the church's image or witness in the pagan society in which they lived is evident in his expression that they should be *"without blemish in the midst of a crooked and perverse generation, among whom you shine as lights in the world."*

By doing this they would testify to the word of life already working in them and would also reflect Jesus' eschatological ministry which included his final return in glory, or his *parousia*. Their living in and for Christ would *endorse the validity of Jesus' ministry.* Paul's final statement *"that* I may be proud that I did not run in vain or labor in vain" reflects Paul's concern for the Philippians.

Paul's comment, *even if I am to be poured as a libation upon the sacrificial offering of your faith, I am glad and rejoice with you all,* raises some interesting thoughts! Paul drew a comparison between his imprisonment as a willing sacrifice to God for the Philippians, and their willing sacrificial gift to him which he had graciously received and upon which he will speak later at Phil 4:10ff. O'Brien observes:

> The language now changes to that of sacrifice (σπένδομαι, θυσία, and λειτουργία) as Paul depicts the life of the Philippian congregation as an offering acceptable to God. To this his own life may be added as a modest drink offering. Although he hopes for a favorable decision from the imperial court, he might instead be sentenced to death. Accordingly, if one thing remains to make the Philippians' sacrificial service perfectly acceptable to God, he is willing that his own life be sacrificed as a libation and credited to their account. There is thus every reason for mutual joy: he rejoices because God has been willing to use him for the sake of the Philippians in the fulfilment of his apostolic struggle for the gospel, while their sacrificial service was something that they joyfully offered to the living God.[8]

---

[8] O'Brien, *op. cit.*, p. 301.

The Christian Example of Timothy and Epaphroditus, and Paul's Concern for Epaphroditus: Phil 2:19-30

[19] I hope in the Lord Jesus to send Timothy to you soon, so that I may be cheered by news of you. [20] I have no one like him, who will be genuinely anxious for your welfare. [21] They all look after their own interests, not those of Jesus Christ. [22] But Timothy's worth you know, how as a son with a father he has served with me in the gospel. [23] I hope therefore to send him just as soon as I see how it will go with me; [24] and I trust in the Lord that shortly I myself shall come also.

[25] I have thought it necessary to send to you Epaphroditus my brother and fellow worker and fellow soldier, and your messenger and minister to my need, [26] for he has been longing for you all, and has been distressed because you heard that he was ill. [27] Indeed he was ill, near to death. But God had mercy on him, and not only on him but on me also, lest I should have sorrow upon sorrow. [28] I am the more eager to send him, therefore, that you may rejoice at seeing him again, and that I may be less anxious. [29] So receive him in the Lord with all joy; and honor such men, [30] for he nearly died for the work of Christ, risking his life to complete your service to me.

After Paul had developed his theme of the importance and joy that comes from Christian service, first using himself as an example, and then Jesus Christ, he then turned to Timothy as an outstanding example of such Christian service, emphasizing the importance of service at the core of Christian faith. Paul's statement is striking! Of all of the fine Christian fellow-ministers that had accompanied Paul, for some reason on this occasion he singled out Timothy as an exemplary servant. Considerable discussion has flowed from this statement! Several possibilities surface. Hawthorne and Martin comment:

> Apparently Paul knew that the Philippians would question his sending Timothy. Timothy seems to have played no significant role in founding the church at Philippi, although he was with Paul at that time (Acts 16). And it is conceivable that in the eyes of the Philippians he even may have contributed

negatively to that mission. The book of Acts is strikingly silent about Timothy at Philippi while loudly proclaiming the activity of Paul and Silas (Acts 16). And although Timothy may have visited (or will visit) Philippi on other occasions (Acts 19:21–22; 20:3–6), no descriptive account is made of any of these visits. In any case, Paul felt compelled elaborately to justify his decision: "I am sending Timothy (1) because (γάρ) I have no one like him, (2) because (γάρ) he, unlike the others, is not chiefly concerned with his own interests, and (3) because (δέ) you know what his real value is to the advancement of the gospel."[9]

The word that Paul used to speak of Timothy's *like-mindedness* or *like-soulness* is interesting, *I have no one like him* ... The Greek reads οὐδένα γὰρ ἔχω ἰσόψυχον, *oudena gar echo isopsuchon* and literally reads "For I have no one equal in soul."[10] O'Brien observes that the adjective ἰσόψυχον in this clause is "a rare poetic word that is found nowhere else in the NT and only once in the LXX (Ps. 54:14), meaning 'of like soul or mind'."[11] After all, Timothy was Paul's son in the gospel (Acts 16:1-5; 1 Tim 1:2) emphasizing *how as a son with a father he has served with me in the gospel*! What Paul was assuring the Philippians regarding Timothy, his young fellow-minister, was that Timothy had the same genuine concern for others as they have seen in Paul.

That Timothy was young says little of his commitment to ministry of Christ. He had a genuine interest in Christ, the gospel, and others. Paul added, some Christians may *"look after their own interests, not those of Jesus Christ. ²² But Timothy's worth you know, how as a son with a father he has served with me in the gospel."*

Paul assured the Philippians that Timothy *will be genuinely anxious for your welfare*.

Regarding Epaphroditus, O'Brien comments on Paul's relationship with Epaphroditus, stressing a profound message to the Philippians regarding holding a *filial relationship of Christian service*. O'Brien observes:

> In a warm and emphatic commendation the apostle employs five terms to express his loving and grateful regard

---

[9] Hawthorne, *ibid.,* pp. 153–154.
[10] O'Brien, *ibid.,* p. 318.
[11] O'Brien, *op. cit.,* p. 318.

for Epaphroditus, who has been a faithful coworker with him in the gospel and an emissary of the Philippians in helping him ...[12]

However, a careful glance at the text reveals more than five expressive or emotive terms regarding Epaphroditus' relationship with Paul and the Philippians. I have set these in bold in the following text for emphasis:

> *I have thought it necessary to send to you Epaphroditus <u>my brother and fellow worker and fellow soldier, and your messenger and minister to my need</u>, [26] for he has been longing for you all, and <u>has been distressed because you heard that he was ill</u>. [27] Indeed he was ill, near to death. But God had mercy on him, and not only on him but on me also, lest I should have sorrow upon sorrow. [28] I am the more eager to send him, therefore, <u>that you may rejoice at seeing him</u> again, and that I may be less anxious. [29] <u>So receive him in the Lord with all joy; and honor such men</u>, [30] for he nearly died for the work of Christ, <u>risking his life to complete your service to me</u>.*

This pericope drives home the theological core of Paul's epistle to the Philippians. They should emulate the example of Christ who emptied himself to become a servant of all; they should recognize this same principle of humble Christian service in Paul and Timothy, and in their own minister, Epaphroditus.

In the next section Paul enlarges on these theological principles and calls upon the Philippians to *rejoice in the Lord*, apparently indicating that joy was not at that time the common experience of the Philippians. He inferred that the reason for this was their tolerance of false teachers and not addressing the breakdown of interpersonal relations among some of the women in the congregation.

Major points to learn from this lesson

1. The Philippians should accomplish/mature their salvation which God in Christ had set in motion. They should do this by completing God's purpose in their lives by bringing their own salvation to maturity in Christian service.
2. They should quit grumbling and complaining.

---

[12] O'Brien, *op. cit.*, p. 330.

3. They should not be concerned for their own interests and should genuinely consider the interests and concerns of others.
4. In addition to Christ and Paul serving as examples for them, they should follow the example of Timothy and Epaphroditus who were good examples of being interested in serving others.
5. The Christians should shine as lights for Christ in their world.

Discussion points from this lesson

1. Discuss what Paul meant by the Philippians bringing their salvation to completion.
2. How can Christians today follow Timothy's example?
3. Who was Epaphroditus? What was his outstanding quality that Paul encouraged the Philippians to emulate?
4. How can we honor these special servant examples in our personal Christian experience?

Chapter 7: Paul's Exhortations for the Philippians

Phil 3:1-21

¹*Finally, my brethren, rejoice in the Lord. To write the same things to you is not irksome to me, and is safe for you.*
²*Look out for the dogs, look out for the evil-workers, look out for those who mutilate the flesh.* ³*For we are the true circumcision, who worship God in spirit, and glory in Christ Jesus, and put no confidence in the flesh.* ⁴*Though I myself have reason for confidence in the flesh also. If any other man thinks he has reason for confidence in the flesh, I have more:* ⁵*circumcised on the eighth day, of the people of Israel, of the tribe of Benjamin, a Hebrew born of Hebrews; as to the law a Pharisee,* ⁶*as to zeal a persecutor of the church, as to righteousness under the law blameless.* ⁷*But whatever gain I had, I counted as loss for the sake of Christ.* ⁸*Indeed I count everything as loss because of the surpassing worth of knowing Christ Jesus my Lord. For his sake I have suffered the loss of all things, and count them as refuse, in order that I may gain Christ* ⁹*and be found in him, not having a righteousness of my own, based on law, but that which is through faith in Christ, the righteousness from God that depends on faith;* ¹⁰*that I may know him and the power of his resurrection, and may share his sufferings, becoming like him in his death,* ¹¹*that if possible I may attain the resurrection from the dead.*
¹²*Not that I have already obtained this or am already perfect; but I press on to make it my own, because Christ Jesus has made me his own.* ¹³*Brethren, I do not consider that I have made it my own; but one thing I do, forgetting what lies behind and straining forward to what lies ahead,* ¹⁴*I press on toward the goal for the prize of the upward call of God in Christ Jesus.* ¹⁵*Let those of us who are mature be thus minded; and if in anything you are otherwise minded, God will reveal that also to you.* ¹⁶*Only let us hold true to what we have attained.*
¹⁷*Brethren, join in imitating me, and mark those who so live as you have an example in us.* ¹⁸*For many, of whom I have*

often told you and now tell you even with tears, live as enemies of the cross of Christ. [19]Their end is destruction, their god is the belly, and they glory in their shame, with minds set on earthly things. [20]But our commonwealth is in heaven, and from it we await a Savior, the Lord Jesus Christ, [21]who will change our lowly body to be like his glorious body, by the power which enables him even to subject all things to himself.

Although there is only a subtle difference in meaning between the terms *encouragement* and *exhortation* the latter term is a little stronger and more urgent than the former.[1] This lies in the sense that *encouragement* lay in the Philippians' *internal* personal spiritual experience of emulating Christ and Paul, while *exhortation* lay in the stern warning concerning the *external* danger of false teachers and external influences.

In addition, the term *finally* in the opening clause does not introduce a final exhortation but adds a heightened sense of urgency leading into the words *look out for the dogs, look out for the evil-workers, look out for those who mutilate the flesh* in Phil 3:2.

Paul's opening statement

Finally, my brethren, rejoice in the Lord. To write the same things to you is not irksome to me, and is safe for you.

Phil 3:1. The word *finally,* τὸ λοιπόν, *to loipón*, derives from the Greek λοιπός, *loipós* which speaks of *something additional or lacking that needs urgent attention, furthermore, in addition.* Hawthorne and Martin observe:

> τὸ λοιπόν, ἀδελφοί μου, χαίρετε ἐν κυρίῳ, "Well then, my brothers, rejoice in the Lord!" Although most translators render τὸ λοιπόν, "well then," as "finally" or "in conclusion" (KJV, RSV, GNB, JB, NIV) and the phrase may on a rare occasion be used to signal the end of a letter (cf. 2 Cor 13:11), the words also serve equally well to mark a transition to a new topic (cf. 1 Thess 4:1; 2 Thess 3:1). Since the integrity of Philippians is assumed here (see Introduction, Integrity of Philippians) and there is no doubt that Paul is introducing new subject matter, it is best, therefore, to translate τὸ λοιπόν as

---

[1] Cf the comment on *parakaléō, entreat, exhort* below and at Phil 4:2.

"and now" (GOODSPEED, KNOX), "furthermore" (Houlden), or "well then" (MOFFATT; see Moule, Idiom-Book, 161–62).[2]
O'Brien adds:

> At 1 Thes. 4:1 this adverbial use of λοιπόν serves to mark the transition from the long thanksgiving period (1:2–3:13) to the παρακαλέω[3]-sentence of 4:1–2, and two entire chapters follow the phrase. Similarly, (τὸ) λοιπόν ought to be rendered by 'well then', 'and so', 'for the rest', 'therefore', or 'moreover' in Acts 27:20; 1 Cor. 1:16; 4:2; 7:29; and 2 Thes. 3:1, rather than 'finally' or 'in conclusion'. How τὸ λοιπόν functions depends on the context. It is clear that new subject matter is being introduced in the following verses; thus we render τὸ λοιπόν as 'well then', 'and so', 'furthermore'.[4]

Moisés Silver adds an interesting thought to his translation of this text. He writes:

> Finally, my brothers, rejoice in the Lord. [There is a matter, however, about which I must remind you.] Writing again to you about the same things is certainly not troublesome to me, while for you it is a safeguard.[5]

I like the thought that Paul is saying to the Philippians, I have encouraged you to mature in your Christian faith *but now, furthermore, I need to add this following urgent message*.

Paul knew that on occasion his imperatival warnings could be irksome to his loved ones, but such concerns for Paul were not irksome, they were necessary, so he continues, now *my brethren, rejoice in the Lord. To write the same things to you is not irksome to me, and is safe for you.*

Gordon Fee notes that whereas it might be irksome to some for Paul to refer repeatedly in his epistles to the danger of Jewish influences creeping into the Christian faith, such as circumcision, Paul found it necessary to constantly warn the churches against this creeping tendency to appeal to the flesh rather than to the spirit, a

---

[2] Hawthorne and Martin, *Philippians*, pp. 172–173.
[3] *Parakaleō* is well translated as *I exhort you*. The RSV translates this at Phil 4:2 as *entreat*. Zodhiates adds, παρακαλέω *parakaleō* ... to call. To aid, help, comfort, encourage. Translated: to comfort, exhort, desire, call for, beseech with a stronger force than *aitéō*, to ask
[4] O'Brien, *ibid*, p. 348.
[5] Moisés Silver, *Philippians*, Grand Rapids: Baker Academics, 2005, Kindle Location, 3837.

contrast he regularly draws on in his arguments against Judaist (cf Paul's epistles to the Galatians, Romans, and Corinthians).[6]

Paul's concern over false teachers

> ²*Look out for the dogs, look out for the evil-workers, look out for those who mutilate the flesh.* ³*For we are the true circumcision, who worship God in spirit, and glory in Christ Jesus, and put no confidence in the flesh.*

Phil 3:2, 3. Paul's striking statement at 3:2 is interesting, dramatic, and stylistically poetical. It is carefully constructed for impact with each clause introduced by the same imperatival verb βλέπετε, *blepete, look out for*, adding a sense of urgency to the statement.

The verb βλέπω, *blépō* is used widely in the New Testament and can suggest several shades of meaning depending on context, each possibility indicating a sense of *look carefully at something*. Zodhiates observes that metaphorically βλέπω, *blépō* can mean:

> to look to, direct the mind upon, consider, take heed; followed by the accusative ... Phil. 3:2 take heed to, keep an eye upon, and thus by implication, meaning beware of.[7]

O'Brien suggests that Paul's sudden outburst with the threefold βλέπετε indicates the apparent threat to the peace of the Philippian church. *Blépō*:

> in the present context indicates some urgency. On balance, we regard the apostle's imperative as a warning that refers to opponents who as yet had not made serious inroads into the life of the congregation."[8]

The poetic aspect of the three clauses is emphasized by the repeated three imperatives, Βλέπετε, *blepete*, each followed by an accusative noun that begins with the Greek letter "*k*" as can be seen in the following text, Βλέπετε τοὺς **κύνας**, βλέπετε τοὺς **κακοὺς** ἐργάτας, βλέπετε τὴν **κατατομήν**. The text translates this as *be on the lookout for dogs, evil-workers*, and *mutilators* (of the flesh). Whereas the first two nouns, *dogs* and *evil-workers* does not necessarily define

---

[6] Gordon D. Fee, *Paul's Letter to the Philippians*, Grand Rapids: Wm B. Eerdmans, 1995, Kindle location 8456 ff.

[7] Zodhiates, *ibid*.

[8] O'Brien, *ibid*, p. 354.

who Paul had in mind, the third, namely the *mutilators* focuses attention on Jewish issues.

O'Brien draws attention to the nature of the third term:

> the third term, κατατομή ('mutilation, cutting'), moves in Jewish categories, so that the apostle's biting irony might designate Jews, Judaizing Christians, or Gentile proselytes circumcised later in life."[9]

As O'Brien observes below, the irony in Paul's argument is that whereas the Jews referred to Gentiles as unclean dogs, here Paul reverses this and implies that it was the Judaisers who were in this case unclean dogs!

The term *dogs* at Phil 3:2 in common parlance at the tie of Paul and the Philippians holds additional thoughts to the irony of Paul's argument! O'Brien comments:

> 'The dogs'. This epithet, which the apostle employs nowhere else, has been given all kinds of pejorative connotations, including impurity, shamelessness, greed, cunning, insolence, intrusiveness, ferocity in attack, and wandering about.[49] It evoked for the Jew the image of uncleanness, for dogs were 'well known for feeding on carrion, filth and garbage'. According to the Mishnah these animals were mentioned with reference to matters of unclean food.[51] The term was an apt description of those who did not submit to Jewish dietary laws and thus were regarded as unholy.[53] 'Dogs' and Gentiles in some contexts were almost synonymous; for example, the Mishnaic interpretation of Ex. 22:31 was that flesh torn in the field could be used to feed dogs or Gentiles ... As a religious term it was applied by Jews to Gentiles or lapsed Jews who were ritually unclean and thus outside the covenant (cf. Mt. 7:6; 15:26–27). Here at Phil. 3:2 the dogs' association with impurity and their being outside the people of God are the points of the comparison. But in an amazing reversal Paul asserts that it is the Judaizers who are to be regarded as Gentiles; they are 'the dogs' who stand outside the covenant blessings.[10]

In keeping with O'Brien, Hawthorne and Martin observe:

---

[9] O'Brien, *op. cit.*, p. 354. Cf also Moisés Silver, *ibid.*, 3809.
[10] O'Brien, *op. cit.*, pp. 354–355.

The Jews were in the habit of referring contemptuously to Gentiles as κύνας, "dogs"—unclean creatures with whom they would not associate if such association could be avoided (cf. Matt 15:21–28; O. Michel, TDNT 3:1101–04; Str-B 1:724–25; 3:621–22). Paul now hurls this term of contempt back "on the heads of its authors" (Caird, 133; cf. Barth, Dibelius, Collange); for to Paul the Jews who promoted their ethnic identity were the real pariahs that defile the holy community, the Christian church, with their erroneous teaching (Jewett, Novum Testamentum 12 [1970] 386).[11]

Paul is not discussing three different forms of corruption in Phil 3:2. The parallel symmetrical poetic construction ties all three together, the dogs, the evil-workers, and the mutilators. As indicated in Phil 3:3 and following, Paul apparently had in mind those who would bind circumcision on the Christians and in Paul's minds they were corruptors of the faith and should be assiduously avoided.

Paul's personal journey into fulness in Christ

Phil 3:4-16

⁴Though I myself have reason for confidence in the flesh also. If any other man thinks he has reason for confidence in the flesh, I have more: ⁵circumcised on the eighth day, of the people of Israel, of the tribe of Benjamin, a Hebrew born of Hebrews; as to the law a Pharisee, ⁶as to zeal a persecutor of the church, as to righteousness under the law blameless. ⁷But whatever gain I had, I counted as loss for the sake of Christ. ⁸Indeed I count everything as loss because of the surpassing worth of knowing Christ Jesus my Lord. For his sake I have suffered the loss of all things, and count them as refuse, in order that I may gain Christ ⁹and be found in him, not having a righteousness of my own, based on law, but that which is through faith in Christ, the righteousness from God that depends on faith; ¹⁰that I may know him and the power of his

---

[11] Hawthorne, G. F., *ibid.*, p. 174. Cf. also Moisés Silver, *ibid.*, Kindle Location 3855.

resurrection, and may share his sufferings, becoming like him in his death, ^{11}that if possible I may attain the resurrection from the dead.

^{12}Not that I have already obtained this or am already perfect; but I press on to make it my own, because Christ Jesus has made me his own. ^{13}Brethren, I do not consider that I have made it my own; but one thing I do, forgetting what lies behind and straining forward to what lies ahead, ^{14}I press on toward the goal for the prize of the upward call of God in Christ Jesus. ^{15}Let those of us who are mature be thus minded; and if in anything you are otherwise minded, God will reveal that also to you. ^{16}Only let us hold true to what we have attained.

Phil 3:3. This text clarified the Jewish issue faced by the Philippians, for Paul writes *for we are the true circumcision, who worship God in spirit, and glory in Christ Jesus, and put no confidence in the flesh.*

Paul referred to his own rich Jewish heritage

Phil 3:4-6. Of all people who could have confidence in the flesh, that is his fleshly heritage as a Jew, Paul believed he would be at the top of any list, but he eschewed such a pride in heritage as a mark of spirituality or relationship with God. Each of the following items alone would testify to his Jewish purity, if such could be attained through the flesh and through Judaism!

^{5}circumcised on the eighth day, of the people of Israel, of the tribe of Benjamin, a Hebrew born of Hebrews; as to the law a Pharisee, ^{6}as to zeal a persecutor of the church, as to righteousness under the law blameless.

Paul's personal decision and goal

Phil 3:7. This text is a transitional statement and will be picked up in greater detail in the following chapter. In Judaism, Paul's "Jewish purity" would guarantee him access into any Jewish society or important position which in the eyes of some would be a great advantage or gain. However, Paul was willing to count them all as *refuse* (Phil 3:8), that he may be found in Christ.

Zodhiates observes that the Greek for *refuse* is σκύβαλον, *skúbalon*. He adds σκύβαλον, *skúbalon; is related to the word dog*, *kúōn which we have already encountered in 3:2*.

However, skúbalon, σκύβαλον, can refer to:
> something thrown to the dogs ... That which is thrown to the dogs, dregs, refuse, what is thrown away as worthless. Spoken of the refuse of grain, chaff, or of a table, of slaughtered animals, of dung, and figuratively of the filth of the mind. In the NT, meaning refuse, things that are worthless (Phil. 3:8).[12]

In contrast to the spiritual realities of faith in Jesus and the gift of the Holy Spirit, the fleshly sign of circumcision is worthless, like *skúbalon*. This had been Paul's theology throughout his apostolic ministry from as early as his epistle to the Galatians. Note Gal 5:1-12, especially his comment at 5:12 regarding mutilating the flesh:

> *[1] For freedom Christ has set us free; stand fast therefore, and do not submit again to a yoke of slavery.*
> *[2] Now I, Paul, say to you that if you receive circumcision, Christ will be of no advantage to you. [3] I testify again to every man who receives circumcision that he is bound to keep the whole law. [4] You are severed from Christ, you who would be justified by the law; you have fallen away from grace. [5] For through the Spirit, by faith, we wait for the hope of righteousness. [6] For in Christ Jesus neither circumcision nor uncircumcision is of any avail, but faith working through love. [7] You were running well; who hindered you from obeying the truth? [8] This persuasion is not from him who calls you. [9] A little leaven leavens the whole lump. [10] I have confidence in the Lord that you will take no other view than mine; and he who is troubling you will bear his judgment, whoever he is. [11] But if I, brethren, still preach circumcision, why am I still persecuted? In that case the stumbling block of the cross has been removed.*
> *[12] I wish those who unsettle you would mutilate themselves!*

A highpoint in this pericope and certainly in Paul's theology and message to the Philippians was *to gain Christ*, be *found in Christ*, and *experience the power of Christ's resurrection*.

Phil 3:8. The following quote from Paul at Phil 3:8-11, is as N. T. Wright likes to observe, a densely packed pericope and one loaded with the high points of Paul's theology, and which will need careful

---

[12] Zodhiates, *ibid.*

unpacking. To draw attention to them I have underlined some of the expressions:

> ⁸*Indeed I count everything as loss <u>because of the surpassing worth of knowing Christ Jesus my Lord</u>. For his sake I have suffered the loss of all things, and count them as refuse, in order that <u>I may gain Christ</u> ⁹<u>and be found in him, not having a righteousness of my own, based on law</u>, but <u>that which is through faith in Christ, the righteousness from God that depends on faith;</u> ¹⁰that <u>I may know him and the power of his resurrection</u>, and <u>may share his sufferings, becoming like him in his death,</u> ¹¹that if possible <u>I may attain the resurrection from the dead</u>.*

This pericope is so loaded and packed with theological emphases that I am devoting the next chapter to unpack its extraordinary impact.

Major points to learn from this lesson

1. A deep relationship with Christ is more important than all other relationships.
2. Knowing Christ, that is having a deep relationship with Christ, and sharing in his resurrection is more important than other religious achievements.
3. Knowing Christ, that is having a deep relationship with Christ, surpasses all other knowledge and relationships.

Discussion points from this lesson

1. Who were the dogs Paul had in mind in this epistle?
2. In Paul's mind, who were the true circumcision who worship God in Spirit?
3. Why does Paul stress joy so often in this epistle, and where does that joy abide?
4. How important is ethnic or family heritage in the Christian life?
5. What is more important to successful living than respected positions in life, or family?
6. How does Rom 6:1-11 fit into this story? What does it stress in regard to having a relationship with Christ?

Chapter 8: Paul's Theology in a Nutshell!
Phil 3:7-16

⁷ But whatever gain I had, I counted as loss for the sake of Christ. ⁸ Indeed I count everything as loss because of the surpassing worth of knowing Christ Jesus my Lord. For his sake I have suffered the loss of all things, and count them as refuse, in order that I may gain Christ ⁹and be found in him, not having a righteousness of my own, based on law, but that which is through faith in Christ, the righteousness from God that depends on faith; ¹⁰that I may know him and the power of his resurrection, and may share his sufferings, becoming like him in his death, ¹¹that if possible I may attain the resurrection from the dead.

¹²Not that I have already obtained this or am already perfect; but I press on to make it my own, because Christ Jesus has made me his own. ¹³Brethren, I do not consider that I have made it my own; but one thing I do, forgetting what lies behind and straining forward to what lies ahead, ¹⁴I press on toward the goal for the prize of the upward call of God in Christ Jesus. ¹⁵Let those of us who are mature be thus minded; and if in anything you are otherwise minded, God will reveal that also to you. ¹⁶Only let us hold true to what we have attained.

In the previous chapter I had set certain expressions of Paul's in bold type which I have repeated above as an outline of what we will be examining as major points in Paul's theology.

As I have stated in the sub-title to this chapter, this represents Paul's theology in a nutshell! In all of the densely packed Pauline texts, and there are many, this one rises to the surface. Without attempting to set these themes in any order of importance the following rise to the surface as we examine this pericope. Paul explains:

⁷ <u>But</u> whatever gain I had, I counted as loss for the sake of Christ. ⁸ Indeed I count everything as loss <u>because of the surpassing worth of knowing Christ Jesus my Lord.</u> For his sake I have suffered the loss of all things, and count them as refuse, in <u>order that I may gain Christ</u> ⁹<u>and be found in him,</u>

> *not having a righteousness of my own, based on law, but that which is through faith in Christ, the righteousness from God that depends on faith;* [10]*that I may know him and the power of his resurrection, and may share his sufferings, becoming like him in his death,* [11]*that if possible I may attain the resurrection from the dead.*

Phil 3:7. The emphatic *but*! Zodhiates observes regarding the *but*, **ἀλλά,** ***allá,*** **it is:**

> an adversative particle originally the neuter plural of *állos*, *other*. It is a particle implying in *speech some diversity or superaddition to what preceded*. It serves, therefore, to mark opposition, antithesis, or transition. It is less frequent in the Septuagint than the NT as there is no corresponding particle in Hebrew. In the NT, it means "but" in various modifications:[1]

Melick notes the increasing emphasis in Paul's arguments introduced by the conjunction, *but*:

> The first side of the comparison is Paul's terminology for his former life. Three times he described it, and *each is progressively more vivid*. First, he considered his gains as loss. The perfect tense form of "considered" (*hēgemai*) suggests a completed evaluation with present effects. He came to realize that they were loss. Second, he continued to affirm that decision. In 3:8 the present tense of "consider" joins with the object "loss." Paul meant that this was a proper appraisal and a good decision. The point receives further emphasis by the repetition of the word "loss" in a verbal form: "I have lost all things." Third, in 3:8 Paul expressed his conviction more firmly with the verb "consider" and the object "rubbish" (*skybala*). There is increasing intensity, as though the mere thought of that decision brought a renewed appraisal that his former life was useless compared to what really mattered.[2]

Hawthorne and Martin draw attention to Paul's radical change in tone or emphasis introduced by this brief conjunction, *but*:

---

[1] Zodhiates, *ibid.*, emphasis IAF.
[2] Melick, *ibid*, p. 131.

Whether or not the conjunction ἀλλά, "but," belongs to the original text [there is a possible textual variant, but the ἀλλά is reasonably well supported, IAF], *there is, nevertheless, a marked transition at this point*. Suddenly all those good things Paul enjoyed, all those advantages he possessed from his parents and from his own efforts that made him proud and self-reliant, are considered now not as assets but as liabilities. Suddenly there is set before the Philippians a startling "re-evaluation [*or*, transvaluation] of values" ... on Paul's part, and any [other] conjunction, however strong, may serve only to weaken *the radicalness of this change in his outlook*. Barthians used to speak of Paul's conversion as "a perpendicular from above" ... which emphasizes the miraculous nature of Paul's radical shift, later theologized as a "new creation" (2 Cor 5:17).[3]

Phil 3:8. The surpassing worth of knowing Christ my Lord. Paul begins this discussion with a comment on the great value of knowing, or having a personal relationship with Christ. Reflect on this for a moment! Rather than having a relationship with the Law, which was uppermost in common Jewish thinking, Paul claimed that one should rather have a deep relationship with the God of the Law through a personal relationship with Jesus Christ, God's wholly divine son!

Furthermore, it was important to Judaism, and thus Christianity, that knowing God, or knowing Jesus Christ, was not simply an intellectual or cognitive experience, but rather something much deeper, a personal and relational experience.

---

[3] Hawthorne and Martin, *ibid.*, p. 188.

Hawthorne and Martin note that "knowledge, then, is not primarily intellectual but experiential."[4] O'Brien adds:

> In the OT knowledge signifies 'living in a close relationship with something or somebody, such a relationship as to cause what may be called communion'. To know God was regarded as of paramount importance (Ho. 6:6; cf. 4:1, 6) and meant to be in a close personal relationship with him. Here at Phil. 3:8 Paul is speaking about 'his own personal relationship with Christ', something that is absolutely basic and fundamental to his being a Christian. It 'includes the experience of being loved by him and loving him in return'.[5]

The remarkable nature of Paul's knowledge of Jesus Christ and God is thus not simply intellectual! But to engage in an intensely personal and relational experience.

O'Brien cites noted scholar F. W. Beard on Paul's use of "τοῦ κυρίου μου, my Lord."

> Beare aptly remarks: 'Here and here alone in his writings do we find the intensely personal Christ Jesus my Lord; and it would be a dull reader indeed who did not mark the warm and deep devotion which breathes through every phrase'. In the Philippian hymn Jesus has already been set forth as 'the Lordly Example' for the readers (2:6–11), and Paul has asserted that God has highly exalted him and graciously given him his own name, that is, κύριος in its most sublime sense, the personal name of Yahweh. On the last day, in honour of Jesus' name of 'Lord', every tongue will openly confess, some gladly but others unwillingly, that Jesus alone has the right to rule and is worthy of all praise and acclaim (vv. 9–11). This same person Paul remarkably calls 'my Lord' (τοῦ κυρίου μου). In using the singular pronoun μου rather than the regular plural 'our' (ἡμῶν), the apostle is in no way suggesting that his relationship with Christ Jesus is an exclusive one. Rather, the wonder of this knowledge of Christ Jesus as his Lord is so great and the relationship is so intensely personal that he focusses upon it in his testimony.[6]

---

[4] Hawthorne and Martin, *op. cit.,* p. 191.
[5] O'Brien, *ibid.,* p. 388.
[6] O'Brien, *op. cit.,* pp. 388–389.

We should add here that in both Judaism and Christianity righteousness was not an experience of being right, but of being in a right relationship with God through Jesus Christ.

Paul enlarged on this; *that I may gain Christ.* On this expression Hawthorne and Martin observe:

> "Finally now, Paul states his motives for counting everything as loss (vv 8c–10). They are (1) that he might gain Christ, (2) that he might be found in Christ, and (3) that he might know Christ and the power of his resurrection.[7]

For many people today, Christians and non-Christians alike, the word *Christ* has become something of a surname or family name of *Jesus, the son of Joseph.* However, *Christ* in the expression *Jesus Christ* refers not to a name but to a *descriptive title*, but to *a powerful theological claim*!

To the Jew, the Greek word *christós*, referred to *an anointed one*, anointed either as a *priest* or a *king*. The Greek word was used in a synonymous reference to the Hebrew *Messiah*. Used regarding Jesus this was *blasphemous*!

For the Jew and the Christian, the words *messiah* or *christós* were loaded theological *sovereign* terms! *Almost a divine appellation!* To the Christian it implied that Jesus was the *Messiah*, the anointed divine king that God had been preparing for centuries since even before his covenant with Abraham. *The Jew thought this to be blasphemous!*

In contrast, this is what the expression Jesus *Christ* means to the Christian! Jesus was the anointed divine Son of God, the chosen and anointed king of God's kingdom.

To come to know Jesus, to have a personal relationship with Jesus through faith was to know God, to have an intense personal relationship with God!

This claim would be disturbing to the leaders of the Jews in Paul's day who had rejected Jesus and crucified him. Likewise, it would be both disturbing and treasonous to the Romans who were concerned over new kings who would challenge their Roman imperial hegemony.

Unfortunately, many Jews consequently rejected the thought that Jesus of Nazareth could be God's sovereign Messiah, the Christ. And

---

[7] Hawthorne and Martin, *ibid*, p. 193.

here in contrast to the Jew's concern for keeping God at a distance, was Paul speaking of having a deep personal relationship with God through Jesus! The Jew kept God at a distance, substituting having a personal relationship with the Law as a means of having a relationship with God! The Jew went to the extreme in that they would not even say the word God or YHWH, and substituted other terms like *Adonai* in favor of YHWH. *Jesus the Christ*, *blasphemy* to the Jew, but awesome and somewhat sobering to the Christian! No wonder that Paul spoke at Phil 2:12 of Christians experiencing fear and trembling when they realized that through Jesus the almighty sovereign YHWH wanted to work in and with them!

Not only was the knowledge of Jesus Christ, which meant having a personal relationship with Jesus Christ surprising, it surpassed every other knowledge or relationship one could imagine such as the knowledge of the Law which had guided Israel now for centuries.

This knowledge was "*surpassing*" simply because it provided an avenue to a personal relationship with almighty divine sovereign ruler of all creation! No wonder Paul was willing to give up whatever he had gained before coming to know Christ! In Jesus, instead of a relationship with Judaism and the Law of Moses, Paul had been granted a personal relationship with the almighty God through faith in God's Son, Jesus the Messiah of God.

The writer of Hebrews expressed this well in several texts beginning with Heb 3:1ff; 4:14ff; 12:18ff:

> *Therefore, holy brethren, who share in a heavenly call, <u>consider Jesus</u>, the apostle and high priest of our confession. ² He was faithful to him who appointed him, just as Moses also was faithful in God's house. ³ Yet <u>Jesus has been counted worthy of as much more glory than Moses as the builder of a house has more honor than the house</u>. ⁴ (For every house is built by someone, but the builder of all things is God.) ⁵ Now Moses was faithful in all God's house as a servant, to testify to the things that were to be spoken later, ⁶ but Christ was faithful over God's house as a son. And we are his house if we hold fast our confidence and pride in our hope ... ¹⁴ Since then we have a great high priest who has passed through the heavens, Jesus, the Son of God, let us hold fast our confession. ¹⁵ For we have not a high priest who is unable to sympathize with our weaknesses, but one who in every respect has been*

tempted as we are, yet without sin. ¹⁶ <u>*Let us then with confidence draw near to the throne of grace*</u>, *that we may receive mercy and find grace to help in time of need ... For you have not come to what may be touched, a blazing fire* [Mt Sinai], *and darkness, and gloom, and a tempest,* ¹⁹ *and the sound of a trumpet, and a voice whose words made the hearers entreat that no further messages be spoken to them.* ²⁰ *For they could not endure the order that was given, "If even a beast touches the mountain, it shall be stoned."* ²¹ *Indeed, so terrifying was the sight that Moses said, "I tremble with fear."* ²² <u>*But you have come to Mount Zion and to the city of the living God, the heavenly Jerusalem, and to innumerable angels in festal gathering,*</u> ²³ <u>*and to the assembly of the first-born who are enrolled in heaven, and to a judge who is God of all, and to the spirits of just men made perfect,*</u> ²⁴ <u>*and to Jesus, the mediator of a new covenant*</u>, *and to the sprinkled blood that speaks more graciously than the blood of Abel.*

Phil 3:9. *That I may be found in him* is a pivotal statement for Paul. Being "in Christ" was one of Paul's dominant theological themes! Cf. Eph 1:3-11 where Paul emphasized that God had predestined us, called us, redeemed us, forgiven us, and made us his children in and through Christ. Paul repeated this kind of statement at least 10 times in that many verses in this text. In Romans and Galatians Paul argued that in Christ and through the faithfulness of Jesus, God had reconciled Christians to himself, he had justified them, declared them not guilty, and brought them into a righteous relationship with himself as his chosen people. They were therefore righteous not in themselves and their ability to keep laws, but through faith in God's forgiveness in Christ.[8]

Paul was not interested in being found in Judaism, in Jerusalem, in the Temple, or in the Law of Moses. He had high regard for the law (cf. Rom 7:12, 14, *the law is holy, just, good,* and *spiritual*), the Temple, and Jerusalem, but Paul knew that it was not in or through the Law or the Temple or Jerusalem that he was justified. It was only through faith in what God and Jesus had achieved on the cross that he had been saved, justified, and brought into a righteous relationship with God. It was only through faith in Jesus Christ, crucified and raised, that God had saved him. He was passionate about being in Christ, for it is in Christ that one becomes an heir of Abraham and of God's covenant with Abraham. To him being a Jew and keeping the

---

[8] Cf. the extensive argument to this effect in N. T. Wright, *Justification*, Downers Grove: InterVarsity Press, 2009, *passim*.

Law of Moses was simply of no ultimate value, it was *refuse* in comparison to knowing Jesus Christ! Cf. Gal 3:23-29:

> *²³ Now before faith came, we were confined under the law, kept under restraint until faith should be revealed. ²⁴ So that the law was our custodian until Christ came, that we might be justified by faith. ²⁵ But now that faith has come, we are no longer under a custodian; ²⁶ <u>for in Christ Jesus you are all sons of God, through faith</u>. ²⁷ <u>For as many of you as were baptized into Christ have put on Christ</u>. ²⁸ There is neither Jew nor Greek, there is neither slave nor free, there is neither male nor female; for you are all one in Christ Jesus. ²⁹ <u>And if you are Christ's, then you are Abraham's offspring, heirs according to promise</u>.*

To be in Christ meant everything to Paul, and he was hoping the Philippians would understand this.

Phil 3:9. Paul's "boast or pride" was that he had no righteousness of his own, based on law and keeping the Law. It has been held by many that the Jewish understanding of righteousness was one grounded in keeping the Law of Moses. This was apparently the claims of the Judaisers in Philippi. Consequently, Paul argued from his own life and experience that in his Jewish heritage, for example in Abraham and David, righteousness came only through faith or trusting in God and Jesus. Serious Jews understood that they were born into a right relationship with God through their birth into the larger family of Abraham's descendants. Circumcision was a sign of such a right relationship with God. Thus Jews made circumcision under the Law of Moses a barrier defining who was in God's family, and who lived in a right relationship with God.

Recent studies from within both Christian and Jewish scholarship have demonstrated that the Jew did not consider law keeping as the means of "salvation" or *entering* a right relationship with God. Keeping the Law of Moses was a sign of *maintaining* a right relationship with God. The Jew understood that he entered that right relationship with God by birth, and maintained that relationship through circumcision and keeping the Law of Moses. Paul, however, argued against the view that a right relationship with God, that is righteousness, was maintained by works of the Law of Moses. Paul knew from personal experience (cf. Rom 7:13-24) that he and others would not, or could not, keep the Law perfectly and thus could never be righteous through keeping the Law. A right relationship with God had always, since Abraham, been through faith in God which now involved faith in God's *Messiah*, Jesus.

So at Phil 3:9 Paul stated that his righteousness, or his right relationship with God, was not one achieved by his keeping law, which he claimed he had done very well. In regard to his keeping the Law he argued that he had in fact been blameless (Phil 3:6). For Paul righteousness had always been *through faith in God*. Now that Christ had come, righteousness was through faith in God's forgiveness found only through faith in Jesus Christ.

For Paul, as demonstrated in both Galatians and Romans, righteousness comes only through faith in God's grace, through the faithfulness of Jesus to God's purpose, and through believing in and trusting in Jesus' death on the cross. Paul believed Jesus' death was God's atoning work to be received only through faith in God's working in Jesus.

Perhaps Paul's clearest statement on the role of the Law, faith in Jesus, and righteousness is seen in Gal 3:16-29:

> *Now the promises were made to Abraham and to his offsprings. It does not say, "And to offsprings," referring to many; but, referring to one, "And to your offspring," which is Christ. [17] This is what I mean: <u>the law, which came four hundred and thirty years afterward, does not annul a covenant previously ratified by God, so as to make the promise void.</u> [18] <u>For if the inheritance is by the law, it is no longer by promise; but God gave it to Abraham by a promise.</u>*
>
> *[19] Why then the law? It was added because of transgressions, <u>till the offspring should come to whom the promise had been made;</u> and it was ordained by angels through an intermediary. [20] Now an intermediary implies more than one; but God is one.*
>
> *[21] <u>Is the law then against the promises of God? Certainly not; for if a law had been given which could make alive, then righteousness would indeed be by the law.</u> [22] But the scripture consigned all things to sin, <u>that what was promised to faith in Jesus Christ might be given to those who believe.</u>*
>
> *[23] Now before faith came, we were confined under the law, kept under restraint until faith should be revealed. [24] So that <u>the law was our custodian until Christ came, that we</u>*

might be justified by faith. ²⁵ *But now that faith has come, we are no longer under a custodian;* ²⁶ *for in Christ Jesus you are all sons of God, through faith.* ²⁷ *For as many of you as were baptized into Christ have put on Christ.* ²⁸ *There is neither Jew nor Greek, there is neither slave nor free, there is neither male nor female; for you are all one in Christ Jesus.* ²⁹ *And if you are Christ's, then you are Abraham's offspring, heirs according to promise.*

Thus, righteousness, or a right relationship with God, comes not through keeping the Law of Moses, but only through faith in God and Jesus Christ, and through living faithfully to Christ.

Phil 3:10, 11. Paul's desire was *that I may know him and the power of his resurrection.* It was through such faith and trust that Paul cast off all personal gain as *refuse.* Paul turned next to the ground of all hope, the resurrection of Jesus Christ. It is only through an intimate relationship with, and faith in Jesus (knowing him), that resurrection means anything.

Paul had argued in 1 Cor 15:12-19 that *unless one believed in the resurrection of Jesus faith was empty and futile.* It was in the death of Jesus that God made atonement for man's sins, but it was in the resurrection of Jesus that God ultimately defeated Satan and gave hope to all that would have faith in his working of God in Jesus, and faithfulness in Christ.

Paul's argument in 1 Corinthians begins with a clear-cut statement of Paul's gospel message. Note again 1 Cor 15:1-5:

¹Now I would remind you, brethren, in what terms I preached to you the gospel, which you received, in which you stand, ²by which you are saved, if you hold it fast—unless you believed in vain.

³For I delivered to you as of first importance what I also received, that Christ died for our sins in accordance with the scriptures, ⁴that he was buried, that he was raised on the third day in accordance with the scriptures ...

Paul had argued at Rom 1:4 that Jesus had been *designated Son of God, powerfully through the operation of the Holy Spirit* in his resurrection from the dead. Later at Rom 8:9-11 Paul wrote:

⁹But you are not in the flesh, you are in the Spirit, if in fact the Spirit of God dwells in you. Any one who does not have the Spirit of Christ does not belong to him. ¹⁰But if Christ

> is in you, although your bodies are dead because of sin, your spirits are alive because of righteousness. ¹¹*If the Spirit of him who raised Jesus from the dead dwells in you, he who raised Christ Jesus from the dead will give life to your mortal bodies also through his Spirit which dwells in you.*

Paul was unfolding in this densely packed text how significant the resurrection of Jesus is to Christian resurrection. He tied both the Christian's and Jesus' resurrection to the working and power of the Holy Spirit. My point in drawing attention to this Rom 8 text is to demonstrate how important the resurrection and the power of the Holy Spirit are to understanding Paul's fundamental theology which he fixed in Jesus' death and resurrection. Christian faith in the working of God in Jesus' death and resurrection are pivotal points in Paul's theology. They certainly are not tangential to understanding Paul's theology as is claimed by some who question the historical and physical resurrection of Jesus!

O'Brien discusses the impact of knowing Christ in a deeper personal relationship as including sharing in and experiencing his suffering, death, and resurrection:

> Paul has already referred to the incomparable value of knowing Christ Jesus his Lord in an intimate, personal way (v. 8). He now enlarges on the meaning of this expression, stating that his ambition is to know Christ fully, something that involved knowing the power of his resurrection and the fellowship of his sufferings in the everyday events of his own life. As Paul participates in Christ's sufferings, the tribulations through which every Christian must pass, so he desires to understand and experience the life-giving power of God, that power which he manifested in raising Christ from the dead, and which he now displays in the new life the Christian receives from the risen Christ and shares with him. Paul enters into a deeper personal relationship with his Lord and thus becomes more like him each day, being continually conformed to Christ's death. This is part of his dying-and-rising-with-Christ teaching, which refers initially to Paul himself but which also applies to all believers.[9]

---

[9] O'Brien, *ibid.*, p. 400.

Phil 3:10. Paul's only desire was *that I may share in his suffering, becoming like him in his death.* For Paul, being in Christ implied not only a blessing but also solidarity with Jesus' suffering and passion.[10] Being united with Christ in baptism (Rom 6:1-11; Col 2:12, 13) infused the suffering, death, and resurrection of the believer with Jesus' passion. Paul was aware that it also involved his own sharing and participating in the suffering service of Jesus. Although the following text can be difficult to grasp and some of it is beyond the purpose of this study, it expresses Paul's view on this point, Col 1:24-29:

> *[24]Now I rejoice in my sufferings for your sake, and in my flesh I complete what is lacking in Christ's afflictions for the sake of his body, that is, the church, [25]of which I became a minister according to the divine office which was given to me for you, to make the word of God fully known, [26]the mystery hidden for ages and generations but now made manifest to his saints. [27]To them God chose to make known how great among the Gentiles are the riches of the glory of this mystery, which is Christ in you, the hope of glory. [28]Him we proclaim, warning every man and teaching every man in all wisdom, that we may present every man mature in Christ. [29]For this I toil, striving with all the energy which he mightily inspires within me.*

The striking point of Paul's comment here is that becoming like Christ in every sense, his suffering, dying, and victory, was the goal of Paul's personal life and ministry, and the heart of his Christian message for others.

Phil 3:11. *That I may attain the resurrection from the dead.* In order to attain the resurrection (that is, share in Jesus' resurrection) from the dead Paul recognized that he needed to be like Christ and in Christ, in every sense of Christ's ministry. He certainly needed the indwelling of the Holy Spirit and the power of Jesus' resurrection in his own life, but he also needed to be fused into the life of and death of Christ, and to strive to be like Christ. His cautionary statement in the next three verses expresses Paul's attitude in becoming like Christ, Phil 3:12-14. Paul recognized that he was on a journey toward the goal to which God had called him.

---

[10] In Christian terminology the word *passion* refers to and synthesizes the suffering, death and resurrection of Jesus.

Phil 3:12. *Not that I have already obtained this or am already perfect.* It is obvious that Paul's pride lay not in his own achievements or personal life. His pride lay in what God had done for him in Christ and in his relationship with Christ. His resurrection came only through his faith in Jesus' death and resurrection which he had demonstrated in his conversion on the road to Damascus and baptism into Christ in Damascus. Note Paul's comments on baptism, the resurrection, and his being in Christ at Rom 6:1-11.

O'Brien adds a corrective comment possibly aimed at a Jewish concept of personal achievement based on human striving:

> Paul has already stated that his supreme desire is to know Christ fully and thus finally to attain to the resurrection from the dead (vv. 8–11). He now introduces a corrective (οὐχ ὅτι, 'not that', v. 12) to remove any possible misunderstanding: he has not yet reached perfection, whatever others might claim for themselves. Instead, he keeps on pursuing this long-cherished ambition with the intention of *laying hold* of it, because the risen Christ powerfully *laid hold* of him on the Damascus road, setting his life in this new direction. There is further progress to be made, and only at the end of the race will he receive the prize.
>
> In his intention to counter the danger of 'a doctrine of obtainable perfection based on Judaizing practices' Paul shows that Christian perfection is a goal to strive for. He has set forth his own life as an example, not in any arrogant way, however, for he knows what it is to struggle against difficulties.
>
> In vv. 12–14 the apostle describes his earnest ambition by means of a series of clauses in contrasting parallelism. The first set consists of negative statements (vv. 12a, 13a) in which Paul's disclaimers are mentioned, while the second set (vv. 12b, 13b–14) focusses on his ongoing determination to fulfil his ultimate aim.[11]

Paul's life purpose was to continue to grow up into the likeness of Christ. Again, the conjunction *but* emphasizes the contrast between personal pride and life purpose. For Paul it was to keep pressing forward to be like Christ in every sense.

---

[11] O'Brien, *op. cit.*, p. 418.

but I press on to make it my own, because <u>Christ Jesus has made me his own</u>. ⁱ³Brethren, I do not consider that I have made it my own; but one thing I do, forgetting what lies behind and straining forward to what lies ahead, ¹⁴I press on toward the goal for the prize of the upward call of God in Christ Jesus.

Paul claimed that the motivating force in his striving to be like Christ was because Christ Jesus has made me his own! He recognized that his life belonged to Christ, for Christ had bought him with his atoning blood. To the Corinthians he had written, 1 Cor 6:19f:

Do you not know that your body is a temple of the Holy Spirit within you, which you have from God? <u>You are not your own;</u> ²⁰<u>you were bought with a price</u>. So glorify God in your body.

Phil 3:14. Paul's goal was motivated by *the upward call of God in Christ Jesus*. The expression *upward call* of God, τῆς ἄνω κλήσεως τοῦ θεοῦ, *tēs anō klēseōs tou theou* is interesting and has generated considerable discussion. I prefer the proposal made by O'Brien:

Finally, κλῆσις has been interpreted of God's act of calling to salvation, with the genitive τῆς ... κλήσεως being understood as subjective (or indicative of belonging). The prize (τὸ βραβεῖον) then refers to that which is announced or promised by the call, and could be a comprehensive expression for the blessings of everlasting life. In the immediate context, however, τὸ βραβεῖον is the full and complete gaining of Christ, for whose sake everything else has been counted loss. The noun κλῆσις, like its cognate verb καλέω, frequently refers to God's initial and effective call to salvation through the gospel: it is a summons to enter the kingdom (cf. 1 Thes. 2:12), Christ's peace (Col. 3:15), or into fellowship with Christ (1 Cor. 1:9), so as to be conformed to the image of Christ (Rom. 8:29–30), and to receive salvation (2 Thes. 2:13–14) and eternal life (1 Tim. 6:12; cf. Eph. 1:18; 4:1, 4; 2 Thes. 1:11; 2 Tim. 1:9). The addition of ἄνω points not so much to the heavenly origin of this call (cf. Heb. 3:1) as to the direction in which this calling leads, that is, 'upwards, heavenwards'. This invitation to enter God's kingdom, which was already issued to Paul at his conversion, is sometimes referred to in the present tense (cf. 1 Thes. 2:12). It is as if the de divine call keeps ringing in the hearer's ears, as God summons Paul and other Christians in a heavenward direction and to holiness of life.

… But on balance we prefer (3), with τὸ βραβεῖον τῆς ἄνω κλήσεως τοῦ θεοῦ ἐν Χριστῷ Ἰησοῦ being rendered 'the prize promised by God's heavenly call in Christ Jesus'. On this view κλῆσις can be understood in its customary Pauline sense of the divine calling to salvation, particularly the initial summons, while the prize is that which is announced by the call. On any view τοῦ θεοῦ indicates that it is God himself who issues the call, while ἐν Χριστῷ Ἰησοῦ probably signifies that it is in the sphere of Christ Jesus himself that this summons is given. In the immediate context the prize (τὸ βραβεῖον) is the full and complete gaining of Christ for whose sake everything else has been counted loss. The greatest reward is to know fully, and so to be in perfect fellowship with, the one who had apprehended Paul on the Damascus road. And this prize Paul wants his readers also to grasp.[12]

Phil 3:15-21. Paul's final statement in this profound theological pericope was to encourage the Philippians to be likeminded and to join him in this quest. Phil 3:15-21 rounds out this concentrated theological piece:

[15]Let those of us who are mature be thus minded; and if in anything you are otherwise minded, God will reveal that also to you. [16]Only let us hold true to what we have attained.

[17]Brethren, join in imitating me, and mark those who so live as you have an example in us. [18]For many, of whom I have often told you and now tell you even with tears, live as enemies of the cross of Christ. [19]Their end is destruction, their god is the belly, and they glory in their shame, with minds set on earthly things. [20]But our commonwealth is in heaven, and from it we await a Savior, the Lord Jesus Christ, [21]who will change our lowly body to be like his glorious body, by the power which enables him even to subject all things to himself.

---

[12] O'Brien, *ibid.*, pp. 432–433; so also Moisés Silva, *ibid.,* Kindle Location 4542 - 4556; contra Hawthorne who sees Christ the prize as in an athletic context. While Hawthorne has a point I prefer O'Brien's conclusion above.

Phil 3:17-19. Paul understood there would be some in the Philippian church who would already be following Christ's example, so he encouraged the church also to passionately follow his and Timothy's example. However, he was also aware that there were some in Philippi who were enemies of the cross. So he encouraged the Philippians to *mark those who so live as you have an example in us*. But who or what did he have in mind in this enigmatic comment?

Considerable debate has been engaged in defining who these enemies of the cross were. O'Brien's suggestion was that they could range from "moral libertinists, behavioural materialists... orthodox Jews, lapsed or apostate Christians—because of persecution ... Jewish Christians for whom the cross had little significance, Judaizers, and so on."[13]

Moisés Silva's comments indicate that there is no consensus regarding who precisely Paul had in mind other than for some reason their behavior was not in keeping with Christ-like living, and whose example was contra to the model of loving Christian concern discussed by Paul in the preceding pericope.[14] Whoever they were, the Philippians knew who Paul had in mind since Paul had previously spoken to the Philippians regarding such persons (cf. Phil 3:18).

> [18] *For many, of whom I have often told you and now tell you even with tears, live as enemies of the cross of Christ.*

Phil 3:19. Without any ambiguity, Paul pronounces a stern judgment on these enemies of the cross.

> [19]*Their end is destruction, their god is the belly, and they glory in their shame, with minds set on earthly things.*

Zodhiates explains that the word *destruction*, ἀπώλεια, *apōleia* derived from *apóllumi* means *to destroy fully* relating in the state after death or exclusion from salvation wherein man, *instead of becoming what he might have been, is lost and totally ruined*.[15]

Phil 3:20. Contrary to the earthly mind of these enemies of the cross, the Christian mindset or *commonwealth* should be set on heavenly things.

Zodhiates observes regarding the concept of *commonwealth*, πολίτευμα, *políteuma* that it:

---

[13] O'Brien, *op. cit.,* p. 453. Hawthorne and Martin, *ibid.,* p. 223 suggest that they could have been simply Jews or Jewish messianic preachers.
[14] Moisés Silva, *ibid.*, Kindle locations 4609 ff.
[15] Zodhiates, *ibid.*, ἀπώλεια, *apōleia*.

derives from the Greek πολίτευμα, *políteuma*. A related word being πολιτεία, *politeía*; which means *to behave or act as a free citizen.* [This involves] *the relation of a free citizen to the state* ... citizenship, the *right* of citizenship ...[to] the state itself, a community, or a commonwealth (Eph. 2:12).[16]

Zodhiates further notes that the verb *politeúō* as we have it in Phil 3:20 means:

> to behave as a citizen of an administration of the state ... In the NT the word can mean the state itself, a community, or simply a commonwealth. It is used metaphorically of Christians in reference to their *spiritual community and their status as citizens of heaven* (Phil. 3:20)."[17]

With the statement that *our commonwealth is in heaven*, Paul was reminding the Philippian Christians that their values should be set by their relationship with Jesus Christ and not by a "their this-worldly profligate earthly mindset." Their values are set *from their heavenly commonwealth* from where they await a Savior, the *Lord Jesus Christ*. I am reminded of Col 3:1, 2:

> *[1] If then you have been raised with Christ, seek the things that are above, where Christ is, seated at the right hand of God. [2] Set your minds on things that are above, not on things that are on earth. [3] For you have died, and your life is hid with Christ in God. [4] When Christ who is our life appears, then you also will appear with him in glory.*

Phil 3:20b. The word order of the expression *Lord Jesus Christ*, κύριον Ἰησοῦν Χριστόν, is significant for it stresses that Jesus, the Messiah, is himself the ultimate Lord, YHWH. *Κύριος, kúrios,* has a wide range of meanings. In the Jewish tradition of the Septuagint Old Testament *Κύριος* was the equivalent of Jehovah, YHWH, which obviously referred to supreme God Almighty. In the Roman context it was a word used to refer to the Caesar, the supreme lord of all that is Roman. In the Christian context it means that *Jesus is the sovereign Messiah, and Lord of God's kingdom.* After all, Jesus shares in every sense the divinity with YHWH![18]

---

[16] Zodhiates, *ibid*. For clarity I have edited or clarified Zodhiates' comments for brevity.

[17] Edited from Zodhiates, *ibid*.

[18] Cf. John 1:1; Heb 1:1-3; Col 1:19, 2:9.

Paul's use of the expression *we await a savior* is interesting! *Savior*, derives from σωτήρ, *sōtḗr,* which simply in this context means *a savior,* not *the Savior which is implied in the RSV by capitalizing Savior!* The word *savior* is in an anarthrus construction which means *a savior* without the definite article *the*. An anarthrus construction identifies *a thing* or *an activity* rather than a name! This text then reads a *savior* rather than *the Savior*. Paul uses the term *savior* in a quasi-apocalyptic eschatological sense and not as Jesus our personal savior. Jesus is the *eschatological savior of all things*, the one who through whom in the end God puts all things right again. O'Brien observes:

> A real parallel is found at 1 Thes. 1:10, where the Saviour (ὁ ῥυόμενος) who is awaited from heaven will effect deliverance from the coming wrath. Paul often employs σωτηρία (see above on 1:19; cf. also σῴζω) in this final or eschatological sense (Rom. 5:9; 1 Cor. 3:15; 5:5; 1 Thes. 5:19), and here σωτήρ is consistent with this usage.[19]

Hawthorne and Martin, along with O'Brien have some interesting thoughts to add the eager awaiting of Christians for the *eschatological* coming of a savior, the Lord Jesus Christ. Hawthorne and Martin write:

> The verb that expresses the church's eager anticipation, ἀπεκδεχόμεθα, "eagerly wait for," is used six times by Paul of the eight times it appears in the NT (Rom 8:19, 23, 25; 1 Cor 1:7; Gal 5:5; Phil 3:20). It is his special word, the one that for him best describes the Christian's persistent yearning for, happy expectation of, and earnest desire for the second coming of Christ, when this travailing creation will be freed from its "thraldom (sic) to decay" … [20]

Note 1 Thess 1:8-10:

> *For not only has the word of the Lord sounded forth from you in Macedonia and Achaia, but your faith in God has gone forth everywhere, so that we need not say anything.* ⁹ *For they themselves report concerning us what a welcome we had among you, and how you turned to God from idols, to serve a living and true God,* ¹⁰ *and to wait for his Son from heaven,*

---

[19] O'Brien, *ibid.*, pp. 462–463.
[20] Hawthorne and Martin, *ibid.*, p. 232.

whom he raised from the dead, Jesus who delivers us from the wrath to come.

O'Brien adds regarding the expression *await*:

ἀπεκδέχομαι ('to await eagerly') expresses 'the expectation of the End'.[118] This verb, which appeared rarely in the Greek world and not at all in the LXX or Josephus, is used by Paul six times out of a total eight NT occurrences (also Heb. 9:28; 1 Pet. 3:20). The contexts are similar, and while the objects of Christians' eager anticipation vary, ἀπεκδέχομαι always focusses on what is definite, future, and eschatological. So Christians eagerly await the revealing of the sons of God (Rom. 8:19), their sonship, here described as the redemption of the body (8:23), the future hope (8:25), the hope of righteousness (Gal. 5:5), the revelation of our Lord Jesus Christ (1 Cor. 1:7), and the Lord Jesus Christ as Savior (Phil. 3:20).

The believers' earnest expectation is focused on the Lord Jesus Christ in his character as σωτήρ ('savior, deliverer'), a designation that is not commonly applied to him in the NT. In fact, the NT makes relatively little use of the term, for it occurs only twenty-four times in all: sixteen of these refer to Christ, eight to God. σωτήρ is not used of ordinary humans. At Phil. 3:20 this saving function has to do with the end time, that is, the final salvation. A real parallel is found at 1 Thes. 1:10, where the Savior (ὁ ῥυόμενος) who is awaited from heaven will effect deliverance from the coming wrath. Paul often employs σωτηρία (see above on 1:19; cf. also σῴζω) in this final or eschatological sense (Rom. 5:9; 1 Cor. 3:15; 5:5; 1 Thes. 5:19), and here σωτήρ is consistent with this usage.[21]

Phil 3:21. With the expression *who will change our lowly body to be like his glorious body, by the power which enables him even to subject all things to himself* Paul again picks up the theme of the *resurrection* of the saints, this time reflecting on statements made at 1 Cor 15:51ff:

Lo! I tell you a mystery. We shall not all sleep, but we shall all be changed, [52] in a moment, in the twinkling of an eye, at the last trumpet. For the trumpet will sound, and the dead

---

[21] O'Brien, *ibid.*, pp. 462–463.

> will be raised imperishable, and we shall be changed. ⁵³ For this perishable nature must put on the imperishable, and this mortal nature must put on immortality. ⁵⁴ When the perishable puts on the imperishable, and the mortal puts on immortality, then shall come to pass the saying that is written:
>
> "Death is swallowed up in victory." ⁵⁵ "O death, where is thy victory?
>
> O death, where is thy sting?" ⁵⁶ The sting of death is sin, and the power of sin is the law. ⁵⁷ But thanks be to God, who gives us the victory through our Lord Jesus Christ.

The remarkable transformation of the human corruptible body into a divine spiritual body like Christ's calls on the miraculous operation of the sovereign power of all the universe, that same power that it took to create everything in the beginning, that brought about Jesus' resurrection from the dead, and in the end will bring everything under God's control. One cannot exclude the power of the Holy Spirit (cf Rom 1:5, 8:9-11) working with Jesus to bring about this transformation. At Eph 4:23, 24, Col 3:10, and 2 Cor 3:18 Paul declared that in Christ Christians are presently being recreated in the image of their creator from one degree to another and that this comes from the Lord who is the Spirit (2 Cor 3:18). Here in the Philippian text Paul declares that this glorious transformation will be brought to fulfillment at the final eschatological coming of the savior of everything, the *Lord Jesus Christ*, involving Jesus' full power of divinity as in YHWH, *God the Father, God the Son, and God the Holy Spirit*!

Major points to learn from this lesson

1. Building off Jesus' example of humility and suffering service for others, as well as Jesus' own personal example of suffering service, and that of Timothy, Epaphroditus and Paul, Paul exhorts the Philippians to join with him and Christ in a spirit of suffering service.
2. Paul laid great stress on knowing Christ and the power of Christ's resurrection.
3. A major point of his message was that joy in the Christian life comes through love for others and a willingness to serve others.

4. The dramatic final eschatological return of Jesus at the end of time, his coming from our commonwealth in heaven, empowers the life and hope of the Christians as they wait anxiously and faithfully for the return of the Lord Jesus Christ.

Discussion points from this lesson

1. Why did Paul choose Timothy as an example of excellence in Christian ministry?
2. What did Paul mean by *righteousness*?
3. What does it mean to *know* Christ?
4. What was Paul's aim in life?
5. How do Christians understand the meaning of their commonwealth?
6. What might have been the teaching of Paul's opponents in Philippi who were enemies of the cross?
7. What was the ultimate destiny of the enemies of the cross, and what does their destruction mean?

Chapter 9: Paul's Final Exhortations to the Philippians.

His Comments Regarding the Philippian Gift, and His Conclusion.

Phil 4:1-23

¹ Therefore, my brethren, whom I love and long for, my joy and crown, stand firm thus in the Lord, my beloved. ² I entreat Eu-odia and I entreat Syntyche to agree in the Lord. ³ And I ask you also, true yokefellow, help these women, for they have labored side by side with me in the gospel together with Clement and the rest of my fellow workers, whose names are in the book of life.

⁴ Rejoice in the Lord always; again I will say, Rejoice.
⁵ Let all men know your forbearance. The Lord is at hand.
⁶ Have no anxiety about anything, but in everything by prayer and supplication with thanksgiving let your requests be made known to God. ⁷ And the peace of God, which passes all understanding, will keep your hearts and your minds in Christ Jesus.

⁸ Finally, brethren, whatever is true, whatever is honorable, whatever is just, whatever is pure, whatever is lovely, whatever is gracious, if there is any excellence, if there is anything worthy of praise, think about these things. ⁹ What you have learned and received and heard and seen in me, do; and the God of peace will be with you.

¹⁰ I rejoice in the Lord greatly that now at length you have revived your concern for me; you were indeed concerned for me, but you had no opportunity. ¹¹ Not that I complain of want; for I have learned, in whatever state I am, to be content. ¹² I know how to be abased, and I know how to abound; in any and all circumstances I have learned the secret of facing plenty and hunger, abundance and want. ¹³ I can do all things in him who strengthens me.

¹⁴ Yet it was kind of you to share my trouble. ¹⁵ And you Philippians yourselves know that in the beginning of the gospel, when I left Macedonia, no church entered into partnership with me in giving and receiving except you only; ⁱ⁶ for even in Thessalonica you sent me help once and again. ¹⁷ Not that I seek the gift; but I seek the fruit which increases to your credit. ¹⁸ I have received full payment, and more; I am filled, having received from Epaphroditus the gifts you sent, a fragrant offering, a sacrifice acceptable and pleasing to God. ¹⁹ And my God will supply every need of yours according to his riches in glory in Christ Jesus. ²⁰ To our God and Father be glory for ever and ever. Amen.

²¹ Greet every saint in Christ Jesus. The brethren who are with me greet you. ²² All the saints greet you, especially those of Caesar's household.

²³ The grace of the Lord Jesus Christ be with your spirit.

Miscellaneous Exhortations

Melick introduces this final section of Paul's epistle to the Philippians with this observation regarding Paul's miscellaneous exhortations:

> Paul's mind turned to various matters in the church. Throughout the epistle there are hints of disunity among the congregation, and Paul countered that disunity with strong doctrinal (2:1–11) and practical (2:12–18) instruction. This chapter presents the only tangible evidence as to what the problem might have been, and the evidence is scarce. Several exhortations occur in these verses: to steadfastness (4:1), to unity (4:2–3), to joy and peace (4:4–7), and to the proper outlook (4:8–9).
>
> Some interpreters question where this section begins. Since 4:1 is obviously transitional, a case may be made for including it in the previous section. Grammatically it is natural for a "so then" (*hōste*) clause to look forward. There is a parallel in 2:12, which, looking forward in the text, applies the truths of Jesus' self-emptying to the church. Here, Paul applied the truths of chpt. 3 to the practical church life. For that reason, 4:1 is included in the exhortations of the final chapter.[1]

---

[1] Melick, *ibid.*, pp. 144–145.

Paul's Final Exhortation: Phil 4:1-9

¹ Therefore, my brethren, whom I love and long for, my joy and crown, stand firm thus in the Lord, my beloved. ² I entreat Eu-odia and I entreat Syntyche to agree in the Lord. ³ And I ask you also, true yokefellow, help these women, for they have labored side by side with me in the gospel together with Clement and the rest of my fellow workers, whose names are in the book of life.

Phil 4:1-3. Paul wasted little time in reaffirming his close filial ties with the Philippians, referring to them as *my brethren, whom I love and long for, my joy and crown*. However, by opening Phil 4:1 with the coordinating conjunction ὥστε, *hŏste, therefore*, he connects this warm statement of brotherly love tightly to the preceding comments regarding the Philippians being members of the commonwealth of heaven. Since the Philippians were co-members of the heavenly community (commonwealth) with Paul this established a firm bond of community fellowship. This is exactly what Paul was encouraging the Philippians to do regarding some of their own members, notably Euodia, Syntyche, and some other of the Philippian church community who apparently were deficient in this regard. The term *yokefellow*, σύζυγε from σύζυγος, *súzugos* raises some interesting possibilities. Súzugos is a masculine noun/adjective from σύζυγος *súzugos*. It has been suggested by some that this was the name of a *fellow male member* of the Philippian congregation. This may be a long stretch and O'Brien observes:

> Who is the person singled out by the expression γνήσιε σύζυγε ('true yokefellow')? Clearly it was unnecessary to name the person (unless Σύζυγε is itself a proper name), since everyone at Philippi, including the one so addressed, would know who was intended ... Apart from a number of fanciful guesses, a suggestion that enjoys considerable support among commentators is that Σύζυγος is a proper name. In favour of this it is argued that Paul nowhere else makes use of this term to describe his official colleagues and that if it were a common noun here it would imply that the person stood in a special relation to him.[24] If Σύζυγος is a proper name, then the adjective γνήσιε indicates that the colleague is rightly named;

Paul is punning, as he does with Onesimus (Philemon. 11; cf. the later Chrestos), and in effect saying: 'You who are Σύζυγος (lit. 'yokefellow') are a comrade not in name only but also in deed' ... It is no longer possible to determine with certainty just whom Paul has in mind; 'faithful partner' suggests a coworker in the apostolic mission who was no doubt well known to the Philippians. He was probably some prominent and influential member of the congregation, perhaps a person of tact[28] as well as influence.[2]

Whoever this *true yokefellow* was, Paul encouraged him to help these two women resolve whatever tension may have existed between them since they had been valuable fellow-workers of Paul and his mission team.

Too often church tensions between two people can develop into serious congregational divisions which can hinder, even cripple the effectiveness of a congregation's witness, particularly in a hostile worldly pagan environment. When earthly this-worldly attitudes impinge on heavenly spiritual attitudes a fractured fellowship is often the natural result. The result set in the context of a "Philippian-type" church is that the church plateaued spiritually, the "blahs" set in, and the joy of Christianity wanes.

Phil 4:4-7. Paul's following comments reinforce his concern that the Philippians may be suffering the "blahs" and a loss of joy in Christ.

> *⁴ Rejoice in the Lord always; again I will say, Rejoice. ⁵ Let all men know your forbearance. The Lord is at hand. ⁶ Have no anxiety about anything, but in everything by prayer and supplication with thanksgiving let your requests be made known to God. ⁷ And the peace of God, which passes all understanding, will keep your hearts and your minds in Christ Jesus.*

Phil 4:4. Paul's use of the double present imperative *Rejoice ... Rejoice*, Χαίρετε, *chairete* ... strengthens Paul's comments regarding the danger of broken fellowship resulting in the church or group

---

[2] O'Brien, *ibid.*, pp. 480–481. Cf. the discussion of this in Hawthorne and Martin, *ibid.*, p. 242; Moisés Silva, *ibid.*, Kindle Location 4932 ff; Gordon D. Fee, *ibid.*, Kindle Location 11177 ff.

plateauing. In Greek the present tense[3] of the imperatival verb Χαίρετε emphasizes that this act of *rejoicing* should be a *constant steady* experience in the Christian fellowship, especially in their shared commonwealth. The root verb of the present imperative χαίρετε *chairete*, is χαίρω, *chairō* which is related to the noun χαρά, *chará* which means *joy*.[4] As mentioned in the opening pericope to this epistle *joy* of the Christian life was obviously high on Paul's agenda. *Rejoice* occurs 9 times in 8 verses in Philippians, and *joy* 5 times in 5 verses. It should be obvious that *joy* in the life of a group or congregation is a primary ingredient of effective fellowship. That joy and rejoice are mentioned 14 times in this short epistle implies that joy was not a present experience in Philippi! It suggests that the congregation was beset with some form of the spiritual blahs!

O'Brien stresses this point:

> Rather, the key to this rejoicing is its being ἐν κυρίῳ [*in the Lord*], 'the governing factor in the exhortation', which signifies that the Lord is either the object of their rejoicing or the ground and the one in whom their joy thrives (see on 3:1). It is just possible that the mention of 'the book of life' in v. 3 induced the apostle to renew his exhortation for his readers to rejoice. Cf. Jesus' words to the Seventy after they returned from their mission 'with joy (μετὰ χαρᾶς)': 'Do not rejoice that the spirits submit to you, but rejoice (χαίρετε) that your names are written in heaven' (Lk. 10:20).
>
> Clearly, continuous rejoicing in the Lord is of great significance to Paul. It is a Christian's distinguishing mark (Rom. 12:12) and a characteristic of the kingdom of God (Rom. 14:17). Along with other graces it is a fruit of the Spirit (Gal. 5:22–23; cf. Rom. 14:17; 1 Thes. 1:6) that will be evident in times of suffering and trial (Rom. 5:3–4; 2 Cor. 6:10; 8:2–3). Because rejoicing in the Lord at all times is so important, the apostle emphatically repeats the injunction: πάλιν ἐρῶ, χαίρετε. 'I have said it once and I will say it again,

---

[3] In Greek grammar the present tense of a verb does not necessarily refer to time, as in the present time. Its primary reference is to the *kind of action implied*, in this case, *continuous action*.

[4] Zodhiates, *ibid*, χαίρετε, *chairete*, present imperative of χαίρω *chairō*.

rejoice!' 'He doubles it to take away the scruple of those who might say, what, shall we rejoice in afflictions?'[5]

A key to joy in Christian fellowship is *forbearance*, a point that in various contexts is high on Paul's paranetic esthetics. The Greek ἐπιεικής, *epieikḗs, forbearance,* in various forms appears often in the New Testament context. It primarily means *mildness* or *gentleness* and speaks directly to inter-personal relationships. O'Brien observes:

> This word group had a long history (from Homer onwards) and described 'a balanced, intelligent, decent outlook in contrast to licentiousness'. ἐπιεικής and ἐπιείκεια were applied to authorities to denote equity and leniency. When strict adherence to the letter of the law would lead to injustice, ἐπιείκεια knew how to act with fairness. In the LXX the word group described the gracious gentleness of God's rule (1 Sa. 12:22; Ps. 86:5; Wis. 12:18), as well as the actions of a king (2 Macc. 9:27), a prophet (2 Ki. 6:3), and a godly person (Wis. 2:19). This last reference is important for two reasons: first, ἐπιεικής is not applied to one with power and authority, and so it does not describe the indulgence of a ruler. Rather, at Wis. 2:19 ὁ δίκαιος, who seems to represent the poor, is delivered up to the whims of the rich and powerful 'ungodly'. Secondly, the context of ill-treatment, torture, and even disgraceful death strongly suggests that ἐπιείκεια here signifies 'a humble, patient steadfastness, which is able to submit to injustice, disgrace and maltreatment without hatred or malice, trusting God in spite of it all'.
>
> Within the NT it is Christ who preeminently displayed this 'gentleness': at 2 Cor. 10:1, Paul speaks of his 'meekness and gentleness'. The combination πρα—της καὶ ἐπιείκεια forms a hendiadys, with the former and better-known term clarifying the meaning of the latter.[25] Elsewhere the overseer is urged to be ἐπιεικής ('gentle') as well as ἄμαχος ('peaceable'; 1 Tim. 3:3; Tit. 3:2), while 'the wisdom from above', according to James, is not only 'pure, peace-loving, full of mercy and good fruit, impartial, and sincere', but also 'gentle' (ἐπιεικής, 3:17). In urging his Philippian readers to 'let their gentleness be evident' the apostle wants them to

---

[5] O'Brien, *ibid.*, p. 486. Comment in [...] by IAF.

display such a Christ-like character, and this may involve them in the patient bearing of abuse.[6]

Phil 4:5. The brief expression *The Lord is at hand* is interesting, loaded, but also challenging! Not that it would surprise one coming from Paul for whom the coming of the Lord Jesus Christ and the presence of the Lord in the Christian's life were major features in his theology.

Note 1 Thess 1:1-10 where many of the themes Paul discussed in Philippians are also found. Professor Abraham Malherbe has suggested that the Thessalonian correspondence in which the eschatological coming of the Lord had major hortatory, ethical, and sociological emphases in addition to the eschatological concerns of the coming *Day of the Lord*, or *the Lord is at hand*. It is in these ethical paranetic and eschatological contexts that Paul brings up the coming of the Lord at Phil 4:5. As an example of Paul's eschatological ethical emphases observe Malherbe on 1 Thess 4:13 – 5:11[7]. In this eschatological context note Paul's comment at 1 Thess 1:9-10:

[9] For they themselves report concerning us what a welcome we had among you, and how you turned to God from idols, to serve a living and true God, [10] and to wait for his Son from heaven, whom he raised from the dead, Jesus who delivers us from the wrath to come.

What may seem surprising is why Paul inserted this short expression regarding the coming of the Lord at Phil 4:5 in the context of repeated emphases on *rejoicing*!

---

[6] O'Brien, *ibid.*, pp. 487–488.
[7] Abraham J. Malherbe, *The Letters to the Thessalonians*, The Anchor Yale Bible Commentaries, 2004, pp. 285ff, *The Parousia and Consolation*. Paul stressed that the Thessalonian's moral character should be motivated and shaped by the presence and coming of the Lord. Professor Wolfhart Pannenberg in similar fashion stressed that *the present should be the arrival of the future* implying that the present should be shaped by one's certainty of the future coming of the Lord. His thoughts are set out in his article, "Appearance as the Arrival of the Future," *Journal of the American Academy of Religion*, Volume XXXV, Issue 2, 1 June 1967, Pages 107–118. The theological, eschatological, ethical emphases play a prominent role in Malherbe's exegesis of Thessalonians. Cf. Abraham J. Malherbe, *Paul and the Thessalonians*, Philadelphia: Fortress Press, 1987; Malherbe, *Social Aspects of Early Christianity*, Philadelphia: Fortress Press, 1983.

Any explanation of the expression is somewhat clouded by what Paul meant by *the Lord is at hand*, ὁ κύριος ἐγγύς, *ho kúrios eggús*. Does he mean *nearby* or *present*, or is he referring to the *expected coming* of the Lord *at the eschatological end of time*. Perhaps both, for both refer to the temporal eschatological end of the world, and both involve the special nearby presence of the Lord. Consequently, both are inherent in the expression *at hand*. O'Brien and Hawthorne have insightful comments on this. Note Hawthorne:

> ὁ κύριος ἐγγύς, "The Lord is near!" Without warning and without any conjunctions to join it either with what precedes or with what follows, Paul suddenly interjects this phrase. Its meaning is rendered elusive by the ambiguity contained in ἐγγύς, "near," which can refer both to space and time. Thus, "the Lord is near" may mean that the Lord is close, present, and hence aware of a person's conduct, concerned about a person's attitude, available to come to a person's aid, and at hand to assist (cf. LXX Pss 33:19 [ET 34:18]; 118:151 [ET 119:151]; 144:18 [ET 145:18]; see Caird, Michaelis, and especially note 1 Clem. 21.3). Or these words may mean that the return of the Lord Jesus Christ is imminent, as in the prayer call Marana tha, "Our Lord, come" (1 Cor 16:22; Rev 22:20; Did. 10:6). There would thus be good reason to rejoice, magnanimously to put up with the harassment of pagans, and to live worry free. It is that the Lord is coming soon to reward the faithful, to punish the evildoers, to heal all ills, and to right all wrongs (cf. 1 Cor 16:22; Heb 10:24–25; Jas 5:8; Rev 1:7; 3:11; 22:20; cf. 2 Thess 1:7–8; Barn. 21.3). Thus the shortness of time and the nearness of salvation heighten the earnestness of the exhortations (Haupt, Dibelius, Bonnard, Beare, Gnilka, Houlden, Martin [1976]; Ridderbos, Paul, 490). It may be wrong, however, to choose between these two interpretations and to remove all ambiguity by translation (cf. GOODSPEED, LB, GNB). Just possibly Paul deliberately chose this particular word, ἐγγύς, "near," with all its ambiguity precisely to include both ideas, of time and of space, together: the Lord who will soon return is the Lord who once came so close to humanity (Phil 2:6–8) as actually to share the human lot and who though absent now in body is still near at hand in his Spirit to guide, instruct, encourage, infuse with strength, assist, transform, and

renew (cf. John 14:12, 16–18, 26; 16:12–13; Rom 8:9–11; 2 Cor 3:17–18; see Collange; Bruce, 117–18; O'Brien, 488–90).[8]

Although the following quote from O'Brien is long and is similar to that of Hawthorne it emphasizes both the spiritual nearness of the Lord, and also the implication of the eschatological end of the age of Christian living:

> ὁ κύριος ἐγγύς. 'The Lord is near'. In the midst of the exhortations of vv. 4–7 (without any conjunction to link it with what precedes or follows) a brief statement of assurance about the nearness of the Lord Jesus appears. Its meaning is not entirely clear because of the ambiguity of the adverb ἐγγύς (is it to be understood spatially or temporally?), while its function within the surrounding imperatives (4:4–7), because of a lack of any grammatical connection, is disputed.
>
> The Greek ἐγγύς, like the English 'near', can be used either spatially or temporally. In the one case, it means 'near, close at hand, in the vicinity', and there are instances of this spatial usage in the NT (Lk. 19:11; Jn. 3:23; 11:18; 19:42; Acts 1:12; Eph. 2:13). In the other, ἐγγύς denotes 'near' in terms of time, and can refer to the proximity of summer (Mt. 24:32; Mk. 13:28; Lk. 21:30), a festival (Jn. 2:13; 6:4; 7:2; 11:55), an appointed time (Mt. 26:18; cf. Rev. 1:3; 22:10), the kingdom (Lk. 21:31), and our salvation (Rom. 13:11). ὁ κύριος ἐγγύς may be understood in a spatial sense to signify that the Lord is close to or present with the Philippians, and so aware of their conduct as well as being able to come to their aid. Certainly his nearness was a recurring assurance to his people in the OT: thus 'He is near' to the brokenhearted (Ps. 34[LXX 33]:18) and 'to all who call upon him' (Ps. 145[144]:18; cf. 119[118]:151). It is possible that Paul is here echoing this OT language,[33] with v. 6 referring to calling in prayer upon this ever-present Lord. Most recent exegetes, however, understand the nearness of the Lord in a temporal sense and take ὁ κύριος ἐγγύς of Jesus' imminent parousia (cf. GNB, 'the Lord is coming soon'). The early Christian cry, Μαρανα θα, ('Come, O Lord', 1 Cor. 16:22; cf. Rev. 22:20), is regarded as a parallel to this short

---

[8] Hawthorne, *ibid.*, pp. 244–245.

formulation, while the words of Phil. 3:20–21, about the readers eagerly awaiting Jesus' return from heaven to transform and fit them for their heavenly heritage, are said to be a fuller affirmation of this great hope. Against the eschatological interpretation it has been argued that whenever ἐγγύς is used in a temporal sense, it is always a time or an event that is near, not a person. However, there seems to be little difference between saying that the *parousia/day* of the Lord is near or that *he* is near. Clearly Paul believed in an imminent advent, *in the sense that it might happen at any time*, and his words are akin to Jesus' direction to his disciples to be 'like servants who are waiting for their master' (Lk. 12:46). But both interpretations are theologically correct, and it may be unnecessary to choose between them. The apostle may have intended to include both ideas of time and space with his use of ἐγγύς: the Lord who may return at any time came near in his incarnation (2:6–8), and is continually near to his people ('at hand', AV) to guide and bless them.

What function does this short formulation, ὁ κύριος ἐγγύς, have within 4:4–7, given that there are no grammatical connections with the surrounding verses? The expression, as we have seen, has usually been interpreted eschatologically, and it is thought to provide the basis or reason for the preceding admonition, 'let your gentleness be known to everybody', v. 5a. *The Philippians are to adopt an unabrasive spirit under provocation because their Lord is coming to vindicate their cause; their gentle response is due neither to weakness nor to an unwillingness to stand their ground*. And, it is claimed, the basis for the apostle's exhortation is similar to that for James's call to his readers: 'be patient and stand firm, *because* (ὅτι) the Lord's coming is near' (5:7–8). Some earlier commentators took the assurance of the Lord's nearness as the 'motive' for *both* the gentleness of v. 5a and the equanimity of spirit of v. 6: the Lord is at hand to right all wrongs, so they should be gentle. His coming will deliver them from all earthly care, and thus they should not be anxious. Other more recent writers, interpreting ὁ κύριος ἐγγύς in a temporal sense, claim that the Lord's imminent return provides the eschatological motivation for all the admonitions of vv. 4–7. *In line with this, J. Ernst has argued that awaiting the parousia was for the apostle a central paraenetic or exhortatory motif. The ordinary things of life, which are referred to in these verses, are important in the light of that return, so that the Christian who has this hope does not live thoughtlessly day by day.*

In our view this confident affirmation about the Lord's nearness, embedded within the series of exhortations, was undoubtedly intended by the apostle to encourage his dear friends at Philippi as he called upon them to rejoice, to let their gentleness be evident to all, and not to be anxious. Although there are no grammatical connections with the preceding and following clauses, the links are provided by the addressees themselves. These believers who are encouraged by this assurance of the Lord's nearness are the same ones who are being exhorted. *For them to know that the Lord is ἐγγύς, in the twofold sense suggested above, namely that he is at hand now and will come quickly, would be a powerful incentive for them to respond to the apostolic injunctions and live in this godly way* (4:4–7).[9]

Phil 4:7. That Paul was primarily concerned with the peace of the Philippian congregation is seen in his expression following at Phil 4:7; *And the peace of God, which passes all understanding, will keep your hearts and your minds in Christ Jesus.*

However, before we get to the peace expression we need to examine the preceding verse Phil 4:6! *Have no anxiety about anything, but in everything by prayer and supplication with thanksgiving let your requests be made known to God.*

We have here a major accent to Paul's theology. *Prayer*! A brief examination of Paul's introductions to his Epistles will reveal a steady emphasis on prayer. Paul prays steadfastly, daily, consistently for the churches and his fellow workers. Sometimes bringing together several different emphases in prayer, *thanksgiving, intercession, supplication*, etc. As elsewhere, here again he mentions *prayer* (basically talking to God), *supplication* (pleading for others or for some concern), and *thanksgiving* (always thanking God for his grace and help) all in the one context. For emphasis, Paul piles up prayer words on top of each other!

---

[9] O'Brien, *ibid.*, pp. 488–490.

Surrendering anxiety to prayer involves turning one's apprehensions and concerns over to God and leaving them with God! It is only when we can do this that the peace that comes from God is possible. Learning to turn things over to God and concentrating on what really is important in life opens the door for the peace that arises out of one's confidence in a right relationship with God.

I am reminded of Jesus' great teaching in the Sermon on the Mount at Matt 6:16-34 where Jesus counselled his disciples not to lay up treasures on earth, but to lay up their treasures in heaven where God is.

> *Do not lay up for yourselves treasures on earth, where moth and rust consume and where thieves break in and steal, [20] but lay up for yourselves treasures in heaven, where neither moth nor rust consumes and where thieves do not break in and steal. [21] For where your treasure is, there will your heart be also.*
>
> [22] *"The eye is the lamp of the body. So, if your eye is sound, your whole body will be full of light; [23] but if your eye is not sound, your whole body will be full of darkness. If then the light in you is darkness, how great is the darkness!*
>
> [24] *"No one can serve two masters; for either he will hate the one and love the other, or he will be devoted to the one and despise the other. You cannot serve God and mammon.*
>
> [25] *"Therefore I tell you, do not be anxious about your life, what you shall eat or what you shall drink, nor about your body, what you shall put on. Is not life more than food, and the body more than clothing? [26] Look at the birds of the air: they neither sow nor reap nor gather into barns, and yet your heavenly Father feeds them. Are you not of more value than they? [27] And which of you by being anxious can add one cubit to his span of life? [28] And why are you anxious about clothing? Consider the lilies of the field, how they grow; they neither toil nor spin; [29] yet I tell you, even Solomon in all his glory was not arrayed like one of these. [30] But if God so clothes the grass of the field, which today is alive and tomorrow is thrown into the oven, will he not much more clothe you, O men of little faith? [31] Therefore do not be anxious, saying, 'What shall we eat?' or 'What shall we drink?' or 'What shall we wear?' [32] For the Gentiles seek all these things; and your heavenly*

Father knows that you need them all. ³³ But seek first his kingdom and his righteousness, and all these things shall be yours as well.
³⁴ "Therefore do not be anxious about tomorrow, for tomorrow will be anxious for itself. Let the day's own trouble be sufficient for the day.

At verse 25 Jesus counselled the disciples to not be anxious about physical needs, and finally at 6:33 he encouraged them rather to *seek first the kingdom of God and his righteousness* and all their anxieties would be taken care of by God.

What is noteworthy in Jesus' final comment is his reference to righteousness which as we have noted previously relates to *a right relationship* with God through Jesus Christ. A right relationship with God, trusting in God, and turning one's anxieties over to God in prayer matures into peace, a peace with God that surpasses all other concepts of peace.

One cannot read this exhortation regarding having no anxiety in the context of Philippians and overlook what Paul discusses at Phil 4:19, *And my God will supply every need of yours according to his riches in glory in Christ Jesus. ²⁰ To our God and Father be glory for ever and ever.* But we will get to that shortly!

At Phil 4:6 Paul thus encourages the Philippians to *let their requests be made to God with thanksgiving.* When Christians do this they enjoy a spirit of peace which can only come from a right relationship with God.

Paul's Six[10] Virtues: Phil 4:8, 9

⁸ Finally, brethren, whatever is true, whatever is honorable, whatever is just, whatever is pure, whatever is lovely, whatever is gracious, if there is any excellence, if there is anything worthy of praise, think about these things. ⁹ What you have learned and received and heard and seen in me, do; and the God of peace will be with you.

Phil 4:8. Did Paul really mean *finally*! Remember Phil 3:1, a previous *finally*! Having said *finally* at Phil 3:1 Paul then went on for

---

[10] Melick has seven virtues, adding *praiseworthy* as the seventh virtue. I prefer to follow O'Brien with six virtues that are *praiseworthy*. O'Brien, *op. cit.*, p. 503; Melick, *ibid*, pp. 150f.

two more chapters! At Phil 3:1 we observed that *finally*, τὸ λοιπόν, *tó loipón* could mean *and so ...*, or *however ...*, or *furthermore ...* where it served as a mark or *point of transition*.

An appropriate translation for *finally* here at Phil 4:8 could read *in addition, my brothers, I have some more to say, whatever is true ...*

Regarding Paul's introduction to the six virtues that follow at Phil 4:8ff Melick adds some interesting thoughts to the discussion of Christian virtues:

> Paul turned his thoughts to providing an environment of peace by unified thought. The church was to make these matters its collective goal, and God would rule in them. Individual Christians were to also conduct their lives in this way. This speaks to the need of rearranging life and thought through discipline so that the God of peace can freely work.
>
> These verses have a definite structure. They contain two lists, each introduced by its own verb. The first list completes a clause with the main verb "think about such things" (*logizesthe*, v. 8). The word means far more than simple thought. The church was to count on these things and to chart its course according to them. The second list completes the verb "put into practice" (*prassete*, v. 9). By using these two verbs, Paul combined the mental and ethical concerns of his Jewish background with Christian thought. For him, knowledge always led to responsible Christian living. Some scholars point out that many secular moral philosophers could have produced the lists since there is little that is distinctive to Christianity. Because Paul seldom used many of these terms, these scholars say he probably borrowed them. Paul may have discovered a list of virtues which was acceptable to him, but the motivations and resources to develop these qualities in a Christian manner come only from the Holy Spirit who produces such fruit within.
>
> Paul addressed the thought life first. He identified seven qualities which should characterize Christians. "True," in the ethical sense as used here, means "truthfulness, dependability." "Noble" translates a rare word which has a broad meaning. Used primarily by Paul in the Pastoral Epistles, it has the idea of "worthy of respect, honor, noble." It is primarily used of church leaders, p 151 where various

persons are urged to be respectable. "Right" is a translation of the Greek *dikaiosynē*, normally translated "just" (KJV). It implies giving to God and people a justness that is worthy of them. This definition differs from Paul's normal use, but it well describes the ideal Christian virtue. "Pure" translates a word meaning "pure" or "holy" in relation to God. "Lovely" is found only here in the New Testament and has a fundamental meaning of "that which calls forth love" (*prosphilē*). It covers a host of qualities but basically means that the person should be attractive, lovable. "Admirable" occurs only here in the New Testament, and it means whatever is "praiseworthy, attractive,"[92] therefore likely not to offend. "Excellent" (*aretē*) means *morally excellent*. The word was seldom used by Paul, but in 1 Pet 2:9 and 2 Pet 1:3, 5 the word describes Christian virtue. Finally, "praiseworthy" means *worthy of praising God*. These characteristics would unite the church and present a good testimony to the world.[11]

At the conclusion of his series of exhortations, Phil 4:4-7, Paul refers to six widely accepted ethical concepts in the Graeco-Roman philosophical world.[12] Whether this list is primarily Pauline, or whether Paul was drawing on an existing list is immaterial. Paul recognized the wide-ranging understanding of virtues already present in the Philippian culture and gave this list a Judeo-Christian motivating twist. Paul urged his readers to let their minds dwell on those qualities which would be good in their own personal lives, but also beneficial to congregational harmony. In a single sentence, using terms that were known in popular moral philosophy, Paul described those characteristics upon which the Philippians were to reflect carefully in order to shape their conduct to be such that peace may mature in their personal and inter-personal relationships.[13] These six commonly known ethical values are identified as *honorable, just, pure, lovely, gracious,* and *excellent*.

I am reminded of Paul's exhortation at Eph 4:29-5:2:
> [29] *Let no evil talk come out of your mouths, but only such as is good for edifying, as fits the occasion, that it may impart*

---

[11] Melick, *ibid*, pp. 150–151.
[12] O'Brien, *ibid*, p, 503.
[13] Cf. Malherbe, *Paul and the Popular Philosophers*, Minneapolis: Fortress Press, 1989.

grace to those who hear. ³⁰ And do not grieve the Holy Spirit of God, in whom you were sealed for the day of redemption. ³¹ Let all bitterness and wrath and anger and clamor and slander be put away from you, with all malice, ³² and be kind to one another, tenderhearted, forgiving one another, as God in Christ forgave you.
¹ Therefore be imitators of God, as beloved children. ² And walk in love, as Christ loved us and gave himself up for us, a fragrant offering and sacrifice to God.

Phil 4:8-9. In Paul's six virtues at Phil 4:8-9 he opens the discussion with whatever is *true*. The noun *true* derives from the Greek ἀληθής, *alēthḗs*, which literally means *without blemish*, or *without anything that can be hidden*.[14] *Truth* carries the sense of being *genuine*, or *someone who can be trusted*.

Honorable is from σεμνός, *semnós* which is related to *sébomai, to worship* or *hold venerable*. Zodhiates adds:

> "*venerable, reverend, reputable, and dignified. Semnós* represents not only earthly dignity ... but that which is derived from a higher citizenship, a heavenly one, which is the possession of all believers. There is something of a majestic and awe–inspiring quality in *semnós* which does not repel but rather invites and attracts (Phil. 4:8; 1 Tim. 3:8, 11; Titus 2:2).[15]

O'Brien has excellent detailed definitions and discussion of the meanings of the six ethical principles of this pericope.[16] For brevity, I have incorporated much of O'Brien's observations in the discussion that follows.

Whatever is *just* has roots in δίκαιος, *díkaios*, which basically means *right, righteous*, and *correct*. It carries a broad sense of *behavior not simply in regard to human right, but also in accordance with the divine standard, and thus fulfilling all obligations to God, others, and themselves. Righteousness* is thus being in a right relationship with God.

Pure from ἁγνός, *hagnós*, is from a verb that meant to stand in awe of someone. It was used in religious language from early times

---

[14] For reference to the individual Greek word meanings, cf. Zodhiates, *ibid.*
[15] Zodhiates, *op. cit.*
[16] For definitions of the words involved in these six ethical principles I have incorporated much from O'Brien, *ibid.*, pp. 504ff.

as an attribute of deity and everything belonging to it; later it was employed in a transferred moral sense of holy or pure ... In the NT ἁγνός appears only in the epistles, meaning 'chaste' (2 Cor. 11:2; Tit. 2:5), 'innocent' (2 Cor. 7:11), and 'morally pure, upright.'[17]

Lovely from προσφιλῆ, *prosphilē*, is a *hapax*[18] word which appears only here in the NT and is not found in the contemporary lists of virtues in the ancient world. The basic meaning of the word is 'that which calls forth love, love-inspiring', and here it has the passive sense of 'lovely, pleasing, agreeable, amiable.'[19]

Gracious, εὔφημα, *euphēma*, is also a NT *hapax* and has been variously rendered as 'auspicious, well-sounding, praiseworthy, attractive, and appealing.'

Having listed the above 6 virtues Paul summarized and reinforced the six in his expression *if there is any excellence, if there is anything worthy of praise, think about these things*. *Excellence*, ἀρετή, *aretē*, ('virtue, excellence, goodness') appears nowhere else in Paul's letters and elsewhere in the NT only at 1 Pet. 2:9; 2 Pet. 1:3, 5 (twice) ... *Praise*, ἔπαινος, *epainos*, signifies the 'praise' that is offered to God ... but here ἔπαινος, or something worthy of praise, in parallelism with ἀρετή, probably denotes the kind of conduct that wins the praise of fellow humans.[20] Paul's encouragement to the Philippians to think on these things certainly addresses the concern he had for the inter-personal problems he had heard were troubling the brethren.

Think about these things in Phil 4:8 is an imperative verb λογίζεσθε which encourages the Philippians to *constantly be thinking* about these things he has mentioned.

Returning at Phil 4:9 to his own example, of which Philippians were well aware, Paul wrote, *What you have learned and received and heard and seen in me, do; and the God of peace will be with you.* Paul is not above using his own example as something to follow since he has already demonstrated his example of living in and for Christ, note his emphasis on this at Phil 3:7-11:

---

[17] I have also referenced O'Brien, *ibid*, pp. 504-505 for most of the following definitions.
[18] *Hapax*, or *hapax legomena* refers to a word or phrase that appears only once in a manuscript, document, or particular area of literature.
[19] O'Brien, *op. cit.*, p. 505.
[20] O'Brien, *op. cit.*, pp. 506–507.

But whatever gain I had, I counted as loss for the sake of Christ. ⁸ Indeed I count everything as loss because of the surpassing worth of knowing Christ Jesus my Lord. For his sake I have suffered the loss of all things, and count them as refuse, in order that I may gain Christ ⁹ and be found in him, not having a righteousness of my own, based on law, but that which is through faith in Christ, the righteousness from God that depends on faith; ¹⁰ that I may know him and the power of his resurrection, and may share his sufferings, becoming like him in his death, ¹¹ that if possible I may attain the resurrection from the dead.

The Conclusio/Epilogue: Paul's Acknowledgement of the Philippian Gift: Phil 4:10-21

¹⁰ I rejoice in the Lord greatly that now at length you have revived your concern for me; you were indeed concerned for me, but you had no opportunity. ¹¹ Not that I complain of want; for I have learned, in whatever state I am, to be content. ¹² I know how to be abased, and I know how to abound; in any and all circumstances I have learned the secret of facing plenty and hunger, abundance and want. ¹³ I can do all things in him who strengthens me.

Phil 4:10. O'Brien's comment opening this section is so important to the overall message of the Epistle that I am including it again![21]

The apostle now turns to one of the main reasons for his writing the letter, namely, to express his gratitude to the Philippians for their generosity, as evidenced in the gift sent through their messenger, Epaphroditus (2:25–30). Although Paul has already alluded to their kindness (1:3, 5) and written with great affection about Epaphroditus, who in bringing their gift had almost died (2:25–30), he does not discuss the gift in detail until now. The position of a 'thank you' note at the end

---

21 I had included it in the Prologue of the Epistle at Phil 1:3ff. Here it is in the Epilogue and concluding part of the inclusio of Phil 1:3ff and Phil 4:10ff. I have set certain expressions in bold for emphasis.

of the letter looks like an afterthought, and this, together with the considerable amount of time that has elapsed between the arrival of Epaphroditus with the gift (2:25–30) and the writing of this note, has suggested to many scholars that 4:10–20 are a separate letter written by Paul soon after he received the gift from the Philippians. But this 'drastic, hypothetical solution' is to be rejected ...

As shown above, the introductory thanksgiving paragraph (1:3–11) functions as a prologue setting the tone and anticipating some of the major themes and motifs that bind the whole letter together. This is particularly true in relation to the epilogue (4:10–20), where interconnecting and thematic links with the prologue are made. The two paragraphs form an inclusion[3] with the affirmation of v. 19 ('My God shall supply all your need ...') and its doxology (v. 20) providing the answer to Paul's intercessory prayer (1:9–11) and the Philippians' other needs as expressed throughout the letter.[22]

Paul's comments resonate with thanksgiving and a gracious spirit emphasizing the point of mutual concern. He recognized that it had not been possible for the Philippians to continue with their original support, *you had no opportunity*, yet they had still been concerned enough to send Epaphroditus to help him in Rome.

Phil 4:13. Paul's remark here is one that has been echoed in the minds and claims of many, unfortunately taking it out of context and beyond what Paul had intended!

> [11]*I have learned, in whatever state I am, to be content.* [12]*I know how to be abased, and I know how to abound; in any and all circumstances I have learned the secret of facing plenty and hunger, abundance and want.* [13]***I can do all things in him who strengthens me***.

What Paul was saying was that in his many trials during his ministry he had been abused and had to face all kinds of difficulties, for example his Philippian imprisonment would have been such a case. On that occasion after having been beaten and thrown into prison as a Roman citizen without a trial he and Silas had spent time praying and singing hymns. The Philippians would have first-hand knowledge about that account! Nevertheless, Paul had learned from

---

[22] O'Brien, *op. cit.*, pp. 513–514.

such occasions that God had always been present with him to give him the strength to endure. Because of God's grace in his life Paul realized that he could face any problem or issue because God always was there to strengthen him.

Phil 4:14. The next pericope expresses gratitude for the Philippians' continued support of Paul to the point of their sending Epaphroditus on the long perilous journey to Rome with a special gift for him.

> *[14] Yet it was kind of you to share my trouble. [15] And you Philippians yourselves know that in the beginning of the gospel, when I left Macedonia, no church entered into partnership with me in giving and receiving except you only; [16] for even in Thessalonica you sent me help once and again. [17] Not that I seek the gift; but I seek the fruit which increases to your credit. [18] I have received full payment, and more; I am filled, having received from Epaphroditus the gifts you sent, a fragrant offering, a sacrifice acceptable and pleasing to God. [19] And my God will supply every need of yours according to his riches in glory in Christ Jesus. [20] To our God and Father be glory for ever and ever. Amen.*

The statement that stands out in this pericope is verse 19, *And my God will supply every need of yours according to his riches in glory in Christ Jesus.*

Many years ago, during my missionary and preaching experience in South Africa I had read through a book of sermons by Charles Haddon Spurgeon, noted English Particular Baptist preacher at the Metropolitan Tabernacle Fellowship hall, 1861. The sermon on Phil 4:19, 20 got my attention! It reflected on Paul's "thank you" comment to the Philippian church for their revived concern and gift. I was so impressed that I adapted it into a sermon for our congregation in Pietermaritzburg, South Africa. I have since preached it on several occasions! Below are the thoughts that stood out for me in the Spurgeon sermon. Paul referred to God as:

1. **My God**, reflecting a *personal relationship* with God.
2. His God could provide **all of our needs**, that is our personal and spiritual *needs*, not our *wants*!
3. Through his **riches in glory**, which are far beyond our imagination, he can and will provide for us.

4. **In Christ Jesus**, all of the real needs that can mount up are fulfilled.

As indicated below in the text of Phil 4:1ff these thoughts tell an astonishingly profound story about Paul and his deep relationship with God and Christ, and with the Philippians.

Paul intentionally and intensely personalizes his relationship with God, it is not simply God who provides Paul's needs, it is *my God*! Too often God is some impersonal power out there somewhere who we call into our lives when we are in need, or a God whom we visit occasionally on Sunday morning! Noted preacher J. B. Philips once proclaimed that the God of many Christians is too small, and one who we call upon in the gaps of our personal lives! Paul's relationship with his God, YHWH, was a deep personal relationship in which he enjoyed God's gracious constant presence in every sector of his life.

God is not limited in his ability to provide for us what we need and is quite able to provide for us out of his abundant riches in glory in Christ. His riches in glory are far greater than any limited church budget or personal ability! God operates out of his riches in glory which are found in Christ Jesus, that is, in a relationship with Christ Jesus.

Fee draws attention to the role in which Christ plays in Paul's theology, and in this letter to the Philippians:

> Paul assures them that God, whom he deliberately designates as my God, will assume responsibility for reciprocity. Thus, picking up the language "my need" from verse 16 and "fill to the full" from verse 18, he promises them that "my God will fill up every need of yours" ...
>
> From his point of view, they obviously have the better of it! First, he promises that God's reciprocation will cover "every need of yours," especially their material needs, as the context demands—but also every other kind of need, as the language demands. One cannot imagine a more fitting way for this letter to conclude, in terms of Paul's final word to them personally. In the midst of their "poverty" (2 Cor 8:2), God will richly supply their material needs. In their present suffering in the face of opposition (1:27-30), God will richly supply what is needed (steadfastness, joy, encouragement). In their need to advance in the faith with one mindset (1:25; 2:1-4; 4:2-3), God will richly supply the grace and humility

necessary for it. In the place of both "grumbling" (2:14) and "anxiety" (4:6) God will be present with them as the "God of peace" (4:7, 9). My God, Paul says, will act for me on your behalf by "filling to the full" all your needs.

And God will do so, Paul says, according to his riches in glory (NIV glorious riches) in Christ Jesus. The Philippians' generosity toward Paul, expressed lavishly at the beginning of verse 18, is exceeded beyond all imagination by the lavish "wealth" of the eternal God, who dwells "in glory" full of riches made available to his own in Christ Jesus. God's riches are those inherent to his being God, Creator and Lord of all; nothing lies outside his rightful ownership and domain. They are his "in glory" in the sense that they exist in the sphere of God's glory, where God dwells in infinite splendor and majesty, the glory that is his as God alone (v. 20). It is according to all of this—not "out of' his riches but "in accordance with this norm," the infinite riches of grace that belong to God's own glory—that God's full supply will come their way to meet their every need. The language is deliberately expansive; after all, Paul is trying to say something concrete about the eternal God and God's relationship to his people.

Which is why the final word is not the heavenly one, "in glory," but the combined earthly and heavenly one, in Christ Jesus. Because Paul has beheld the "glory of God in the face of Christ Jesus" (2 Cor 4:6), expressed in this letter in the majestic Christ narrative in 2:6-11, Paul sees clearly that Christ Jesus is the way God has made his love known and available to his human creatures. This is what the letter has ultimately been all about. It began in Christ Jesus; it now concludes in Christ Jesus. For Paul "to live is Christ and to die is gain." Thus, the final word in the body of the letter proper is this one, "every need of yours according to the wealth that is God's in glory made available to you in Christ Jesus."[23]

O'Brien also expresses this well:

This concluding phrase, like the previous two, is to be taken with the verb πληρώσει, *complete, fulfill*[24], (rather than

---

[23] Fee, *ibid.*, pp. 192ff.
[24] English translation *complete, fulfill* supplied by IAF.

with ἐν δόξῃ) and signifies either the sphere in which God's supplying takes place or, more likely, is instrumental and means 'through Christ Jesus'. Jesus Christ is the one through whom God's marvelous promise for the Philippians will be fulfilled.[25]

Contrary to our desires and sometimes expectations, it is not our *wants* that God meets, but our *needs*, especially our spiritual and emotional needs, but even beyond that, our physical *needs*! When I pray for God to bring healing to my physical body, which I believe he has the power to do, he sometimes does not respond in the manner that I *want*. However, when I pray for him to give me the strength to handle my illness, and for patience and faith to endure the trials of illness, even death, I believe that this is where God shines the brightest. *In Christ Jesus* I have all the assurance I need that God has always acted in my behalf, even since before creation (Eph 1:3-11) with my best interest and needs foremost in mind.

> *Blessed be the God and Father of our Lord Jesus Christ, who has blessed us in Christ with every spiritual blessing in the heavenly places, ⁴ even as he chose us in him before the foundation of the world, that we should be holy and blameless before him. ⁵ He destined us in love to be his sons through Jesus Christ, according to the purpose of his will, ⁶ to the praise of his glorious grace which he freely bestowed on us in the Beloved.*[26]

Paul knew this from personal experience. He had some physical handicap that he had asked God many times to cure but God had a greater purpose in mind, that is, Paul's spiritual and emotional needs. I am sure that you are already ahead of me and recall Paul's comment in this regard at 2 Cor 12:6ff. In the context of discussing his many spiritual revelations and life experiences Paul made the following truly remarkable comment.

> *Though if I wish to boast, I shall not be a fool, for I shall be speaking the truth. But I refrain from it, so that no one may think more of me than he sees in me or hears from me. ⁷ And to keep me from being too elated by the abundance of revelations, a thorn was given me in the flesh, a messenger of Satan, to harass me, to keep me from being too elated. ⁸ Three*

---

[25] O'Brien, *ibid.*, p. 549.
[26] Eph 1:3–6.

times I besought the Lord about this, that it should leave me; ⁹ but he said to me, "My grace is sufficient for you, for my power is made perfect in weakness." I will all the more gladly boast of my weaknesses, that the power of Christ may rest upon me. ¹⁰ For the sake of Christ, then, I am content with weaknesses, insults, hardships, persecutions, and calamities; for when I am weak, then I am strong.

Paul's Closing Doxology: Phil 4:20

Phil 4:20. So profound is the last statement of Phil 4:19 that without anything more to say Paul bursts forth with praise of the glory of God. *To our God and Father be glory for ever and ever. Amen.*

Note especially again Paul's personalization of his relationship with God. This God is not only his God, but he is also the God of the Philippians; *our God.*

In Paul's letter to the Ephesians Paul argued that Christians have been called and destined since before the foundation of the world to be God's children in Christ and to so live their lives that they bring glory to God in Christ Jesus and the church (Eph 1:3-14). Now in his final doxology to this he closes his epistle to the Philippians with a prayer that everything covered in the letter would turn out to the glory of God.

To this he adds the traditional *amen.* Zodhiates observes:
> The Greek ἀμήν, *amḗn*; is transliterated from the Hebrew 'āmēn ... Amen, to be firm, steady, truthworthy. It is rendered also as "truth" (Is. 65:16, "God of amen"; Jer. 11:5, "So be it").[27]

O'Brien sums up the discussion on the doxology and Amen well:
> The spontaneous endorsement of this doxology is uttered in the ἀμήν ('amen, truly, so let it be') that follows. 'Amen' was said on solemn occasions in the OT to confirm a curse or adjuration, to accept a blessing, or to associate oneself with a doxology. Each of the doxologies that concludes the first four books of the OT psalter (Pss. 41:13; 72:19; 89:52; 106:48) ends with an ἀμήν, while prayers and doxologies in the NT are strengthened and endorsed by it. This 'Amen' makes it clear that Paul's ascription of praise is not simply a matter of the

---

[27] Zodhiates, *ibid.*

lips or of the 'pen', but is the spontaneous response of his whole being. Elsewhere he strikingly connects believers' response of ἀμήν to the faithfulness of God, who has said 'Yes' to all his promises in Christ (2 Cor. 1:20).[28]

Paul's Final Greetings: Phil 4:21-23

[21] Greet every saint in Christ Jesus. The brethren who are with me greet you. [22] All the saints greet you, especially those of Caesar's household.
[23] The grace of the Lord Jesus Christ be with your spirit.

Phil 4:21, 22. Note again the mention of the *saints* (ἅγιος, *hágios*) a specialized term for those who have been sanctified (the verb being *hagiázō*) in Christ through His shed blood and their obedience in faith to the gospel of Christ. Paul had opened the epistle with an emphasis on all who were saints, *Paul and Timothy, servants of Christ Jesus, to all the saints in Christ Jesus who are at Philippi, with the bishops and deacons*, and now he closes the epistle on the same note, *greet every saint*.

The fact that the term saint is a special term for those who have been cleansed by the blood of Christ, and through this have been brought into a special relationship with God, adds to the significant thought that *the Philippians are saints and need to act like saints*, which has been a theme of the Epistle!

The remainder of this greeting includes those who are associated with Paul in his Roman experience, even some in Caesar's household, *the brethren who are with me greet you. [22] All the saints greet you, especially those of Caesar's household.*

O'Brien draws attention to the depth of this greeting and conclusion:

> Paul sends his own and his coworkers' greetings to each one of God's people at Philippi. It was probably the 'church leaders and helpers' (1:1) who would see that the letter was read to the whole congregation and greetings conveyed to all.
>
> ἀσπάσασθε πάντα ἅγιον ἐν Χριστῷ Ἰησοῦ. 'Give my greetings to each member of God's people in Christ Jesus'. Paul's final greeting is striking: (1) the verb ἀσπάσασθε is an imperative in the second person plural ('you [pl.] give my

---

[28] O'Brien, *ibid.*, p. 550.

greetings'), addressed not to the church as a whole but to certain individuals within it who are to pass on his greeting to others. Although it is not certain to whom this injunction is addressed, probably the 'church leaders and helpers' (1:1) are in mind. Presumably they would see that the letter was read and greetings conveyed to all the members of the Philippian church. ἀσπάζομαι 'greet', the basic meaning of which seems to be 'embrace') is the normal term used of greeting in the NT. Forty-seven of its sixty occurrences are in epistolary formulas. It turns up in almost all the letters, appearing in two forms: (a) an *imperative*, in which the writer asks his readers to present his greetings from a distance, or sends a greeting to all the members of the community (cf. πάντα ἅγιον here). (b) An *indicative* (such as ἀσπάζονται) is used when fellow Christians are absent at the time of writing. Paul passes on their greetings and either mentions them by name or refers to them generally (as here).[7] These greetings help to give the readers a clear picture of the circumstances in which the letter was written and to include friends and coworkers of the apostle in the fellowship he enjoys with the readers.

(2) The second unusual feature of this greeting is the singular form, πάντα ἅγιον ἐν Χριστῷ Ἰησοῦ (lit. 'every saint in Christ Jesus'),[9] used to describe the recipients. In his love and care for them Paul sends his greetings to every member of the congregation. He wants all the Lord's people to know that he remembers them individually. Each one of them is 'a holy one' (ἅγιος) who is stamped with the seal of being in Christ Jesus. This emphasis may also explain the surprising omission of personal names in these final verses. It is striking that to a church with whom the apostle had the warmest of relations, contrary to his usual custom, he makes no mention of a Lydia, a Philippian jailer, or others. Perhaps some special greetings may have been sent through Epaphroditus, the bearer of the letter. But Paul may have omitted all personal salutations so as not to give any suggestion of partiality, especially since he had mentioned to them their need to be united (2:1–4; 4:3) and to follow the Lord's example of showing humility to one another (2:5–11).

ἀσπάζονται ὑμᾶς οἱ σὺν ἐμοὶ ἀδελφοί. 'The brothers who are with me here send you their greetings'. This group, which is narrower than those described as 'all God's people' (πάντες οἱ ἅγιοι, v. 22), probably refers to Paul's companions or coworkers, who were intimately involved with him in his ministry. It would no doubt have included Timothy (cf. 1:1; 2:19–24) and possibly also Luke (cf. Acts 27:1), though how large the circle was we do not know.[29]

Phil 4:23. Paul closes with a prayer that the Philippians may experience the grace/favor of the Lord Jesus Christ and that the grace of the Lord Jesus Christ would be with them in spirit, or in their innermost being, their hearts as a seat of deep emotions. However, Hawthorne observes:

> Paul begins his letter with χάρις, "grace" (Phil 1:2); he now concludes it with that same rich word. With few exceptions (Col 1:2; 1 Thess 1:1), whenever Paul begins his letters, he speaks of "the grace of God our Father and of the Lord Jesus Christ." With equally few exceptions (Eph 6:23; 1 Tim 6:21; 2 Tim 4:22; Tit 3:15 within the Pauline corpus), in the benediction at the close of these same letters Paul only speaks of the grace of the Lord Jesus Christ. This fact leads one to conclude that for Paul Christ has the right to perform the divine role with full authority. He is the source of grace, the fountainhead of free beneficent saving love (χάρις, "grace"). He is the one who bestows this grace freely on his church. He is the one through whom undeserving humankind comes to know the mercy, love, and favor of God. He is the Lord whom the church confesses ...
>
> Paul's final benediction ... then, is that this grace of Jesus Christ as Lord may be μετὰ τοῦ πνεύματος ὑμῶν, lit. "with your spirit." This expression sounds strange to modern ears. Thus, several things should be noted: (1) The fact that πνεύματος, "spirit," is singular and ὑμῶν, "your," is plural does not necessarily lead to the conclusion that Paul is stressing "the unity of the body of believers in which one spirit is to be found" ... The distributive singular—as in πεπωρωμένην ἔχετε τὴν καρδίαν ὑμῶν, "you [plural] have a

---

[29] O'Brien, *ibid.*, pp. 552–554.

hardened heart" (Mark 8:17), meaning, "each of you has a hardened heart"—is a common enough phenomenon in both classical and NT Greek ... Hence the singular here has no significant meaning beyond the fact that Paul's prayer is for Christ's grace to rest and abide upon the spirit of *each one* of his readers ... (2) The word πνεῦμα, "spirit," is frequently used in the NT of the whole person, but especially of the mental and spiritual aspects belonging to personality ... (3) The phrase μετὰ τοῦ πνεύματος ὑμῶν, "with your spirit," is not unique to Philippians ... it appears also in Gal 6:18; Phlm 25 (cf. 2 Tim 4:22). It stands in the same position in these benedictions as—and replaces the more usual—μεθ' ὑμῶν, "with you." (4) Hence in all likelihood Paul means to say nothing more profound by the expression "with your spirit" than to say "with you." It should thus be translated accordingly.[30]

Major points to learn from this lesson

1. Paul graciously acknowledges the Philippians' concern for him and the gift Epaphroditus, their minister, had brought to him in Rome.
2. The message builds on the point Paul had been making - joy in Christianity is experienced in Christian concern for others and Christ-like service.
3. Paul stressed that he had learned from his experiences that God always took care of him and in this knowledge, he could live through both good and bad experiences through faith in God.
4. God is capable of taking care of us out of his riches in glory in Christ.

Discussion points from this lesson

1. Discuss what Paul meant by claiming that he could do all things through Christ/God who strengthens him.
2. What is the secret of facing plenty and hunger, abundance and want?

---

[30] Hawthorne, *ibid.* pp. 281–282.

3. How could this be true if Paul had been beaten and jailed in Philippi and was in prison in Rome when he wrote the letter to the Philippians?
4. What is the difference between what we want and what we need? Who is the best judge in such matters?

AUTHOR

Ian A. Fair (PhD)
Professor Emeritus of New Testament
and New Testament Theology
Graduate School of Theology
College of Biblical Studies
Abilene Christian University

TEACHING & SPECIALIZATION	SEMINARS AND WORKSHOPS
Revelation	Revelation
Romans	Romans
Prison Epistles	Matthew
Synoptic Gospels: Matthew	Strategic Planning
1 & 2 Thessalonians	Leadership
Leadership	Unity in Diversity

Education
Ph.D. in Systematic Theology, University of Natal, South Africa
Dissertation: *The Theology of Wolfhart Pannenberg as a Reaction to Dialectical Theology*
MA in New Testament Theology, University of Natal, South Africa
Thesis: *The Resurrection of Jesus in Three Contemporary Theologians*
BA Honors in Bible and Theology, University of Natal, South Africa
BA in Bible, Abilene Christian University, Abilene, Texas, USA.

WHO WE ARE

HCU Media LLC

Publishing in support of

Heritage Christian University – Ghana (HCU Ghana)

www.hcuc.edu.gh

HCU media has been established to support the publication of materials, both paper and electronic, created by faculty and friends of HCU Ghana. These materials will be offered initially in the USA & Ghana but may become available globally via other outlets.

www.ingramcontent.com/pod-product-compliance
Lightning Source LLC
Chambersburg PA
CBHW030116100526
44591CB00009B/422